The Art and Science

of

Real Wealth

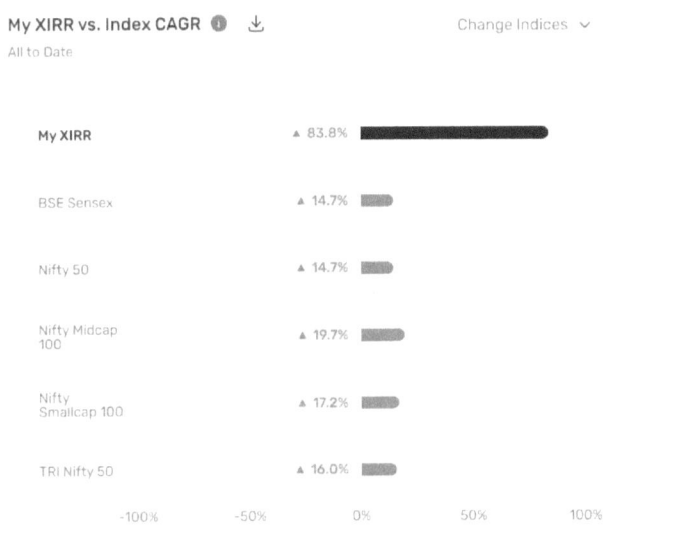

My XIRR vs. Index CAGR ⓘ ⤓

Change Indices ⌄

All to Date

My XIRR	▲ 83.8%
BSE Sensex	▲ 14.7%
Nifty 50	▲ 14.7%
Nifty Midcap 100	▲ 19.7%
Nifty Smallcap 100	▲ 17.2%
TRi Nifty 50	▲ 16.0%

-100% -50% 0% 50% 100%

5 Year 83% XIRR from FY 20-21 to August 9, 2024

Dhyan Appachu Bollachettira

Author : Arya Dharma: The Noble Dharma

लोकाः समस्ताः सुखिनोभवन्तु

Lokah Samastah Sukhino Bhavantu

May all the Worlds become Happy.

DHYAN KUTAPPA BOLLACHETTIRA

This publication is for informational purposes only, it should not be considered Financial or Legal Advice.

Consult a financial professional before making any major financial decisions.

Before you take their advice, make sure the financial professional has a significant portion of their own, and if possible also their spouse and children's net worth, in the investments that they are recommending to you, just like I have done, and publicly displayed at   *www.artofrealwealth.com*

Contents

Preface

Where the mind is without fear and the head is held high

Where knowledge is free

Where the world has not been broken up into fragments by narrow domestic walls

Where words come out from the depth of truth

Where tireless striving stretches its arms towards perfection

Where the clear stream of reason has not lost its way into the dreary desert sand of dead habit

Where the mind is led forward by thee into ever-widening thought and action

Into that heaven of freedom, my Father, let my country awake.

Rabindranath Tagore

The Purpose of this Publication

I have been in the field of investing ever since I was a young teen during the mania of the early 1990s. I have had huge successes and even bigger failures and after that until date (October 2024) even bigger successes again.

I made enough money before I was 30 (2004), that ordinary people would not have made in a lifetime.

If I had just done my first investment as a young teen in life, in the mania of the early 1990s, based on logic, patience and reason, and more importantly on a trusted friend's advice instead of a crooked broker's stock tip, in MRF, and not on emotion and mania, and no other investment, I would have had more than Rs 590 crores (79 million dollars) by June 2020.

If I just stopped investing at 30 (2004), taken all my winnings and only bought Apple, I would have had almost than 27 million dollars (Rs 202 crores) by June 2020.

But my short-term emotional thinking, arrogance, and greed in investing, and ignoring and mocking the principles of capital allocation and risk management blew away all those earnings.

I used to think only for the next 3 months while investing.

Now I have a vision of at least 5 years. For stocks that I missed out like what I mentioned above, I have a vision of 15+ years.

For an investment to really pay off you need to be patient and disciplined.

The world's greatest investors were successful only because of logic, reason, patience, and discipline.

Another important thing is that you should never fall in love with your investment in material assets.

If your investment in material assets starts to fall beyond a certain limit or is causing you to bleed from your pockets just sell it.

Like the saying goes:

Money goes and comes again

So even though I have lost huge amounts of money that I made myself, due to arrogance, greed and stupidity, since 2018, I changed my whole strategy and reviewed my life's experience since I started actively investing as a young teen in the early 1990s.

This change in strategy and more importantly the strengthening of my mind due to consistent practice of ध्यान Dhyana since 2015 has made me a very mentally strong and disciplined individual and now I would like to believe I am beyond ignorance, fear, hope and greed while investing and I hope at most things that life throws at me.

One who masters ignorance, fear, hope and greed will conquer himself and as Paulo Coelho said:

If you conquer yourself, then you will conquer the world.

I thought I should share my life's learning over the last 31 years in the art and science of investing.

I hope it prevents others from making the mistakes I made until 2018, and straightaway skip all my mistakes and go on to the success I am having since 2019.

I always had a gift for strategic thinking and problem solving.

This has been a real curse, since I fared rather poorly academically, because I only depended on my inborn God given genetic lottery inherited skills, and not on discipline, consistency and hard work which are also required to achieve academic distinction or distinction in any field of life.

In fact, in the Mettl Psychometric Test I took at my last company, I scored a 10/10 in both strategic thinking and problem solving, an 8/10 on ethical propensity and accountability and a 9/10 on resilience.

We should use something like the Mettl Psychometric Test before we decided to engage and do business with all Representative DFIs, corrupt Sarkari babus, and Wall Street/Dalal Street Pimps and Lalas.

Only if they score at least a 7/10 on strategic thinking, problem solving, accountability and ethical propensity, should we give them roles of great power and influence.

Otherwise we should just give them jobs of digging ditches, breaking stones and cleaning manholes which are the only jobs most Representative DFIs, corrupt Sarkari babus, and Wall Street/Dalal Street Pimps and Lalas are actually underqualified to do.

An 8/10 on accountability is not a bad score. Only Bhishma would have scored a 10/10 and that's why he ended up lying on a bed of arrows for 58 days and on the wicked and losing side.

Only Jesus Christ and Lord Ram will score a 10/10 on ethical propensity and look at the trouble they got into.

An 8/10 on ethical propensity is also a decent score but as Kautilya said:

One should not be too straightforward.

Go and see the forest.

The straight trees are cut down, the crooked ones are left standing.

I am not a crooked tree.

I never lie, cheat and steal and will always honour a promise, even a verbal promise.

But sometimes, I will not disclose things unless I am asked about it, even if the right thing to do was to be upfront and disclose it.

The purpose of this publication is to enable you to manage money wisely and earn a consistent regular income. This publication will enable you to achieve financial freedom.

But this publication has a higher purpose. To get you to read my book Arya Dharma: The Noble Dharma.

Read the reader reviews regarding my book Arya Dharma.

My book Arya Dharma: The Noble Dharma is my life's dream and will enable to you achieve Moksha or freedom from the permanent influence of करम Karma or Destiny.

You don't have to buy the book if you cannot afford it, there is a free download available from my website www.aryadharma.world.

In fact, you don't even have to buy this publication if you cannot afford it, there is a free version available for download at www.artofrealwealth.com

The purpose of wealth is not to buy large mansions and fancy cars and waste it on superfluous extravagance, toy boys, mistresses and undeserving charities meant only for the fish love of furthering your dreams.

The purpose of wealth is to give you the freedom to pursue your higher passions and more importantly discover the joys of SEVA (Selfless Service) by helping the most needy and unfortunate beings in this world by giving them true love and the ability to chase their dreams, not yours.

The highest goal of the Arthasastra is SEVA to the old – the highest ideal of Dharma.

DHYAN KUTAPPA BOLLACHETTIRA

सुखस्य मूलं धर्मः । धर्मस्य मूलं अर्थः । अर्थस्य मूलं राज्यं । राज्यस्य मूलं इन्द्रिय जयः । इन्द्रियजयस्य मूलं विनियः । विनियस्य मूलं वृद्धोपसेवा॥

The root of happiness and wellbeing
is Dharma.
The root of Dharma is Artha (economy and
statecraft or wealth)
The root of Artha is good governance.
The root of good governance is conquering by
self-control.
The root of conquering by self-control is
humility.
The root of humility is SEVA (selfless
service) to the old.

My main intention to write this book and the website www.aryadharma.world is to change world consciousness and governments to a better way of life and living and to restore the Arya Dharma – the Noble Dharma not only for humanity but for all beings in this world.

I still remember the golden words of my Dad's friend Mr Swami:

In the Vedanta, I find peace.

This small and profound sentence that I heard when I was a young child was spark for me to embark on my journey into finding peace and I wish to share with the world what I have found.

DHYAN KUTAPPA BOLLACHETTIRA

Introduction

According to me, the difference between an investor and a speculator is that a speculator is only interested in return on financial capital.

So, in some way all of us are just speculators if all we are looking for is return on financial capital.

An investor is someone who invests in a business hands on, not just buying shares in the stock market.

An investor will research the business, be an active participant and will be interested in the business as a whole.

Not just its profits and revenues, but also its employees, its clients, and its positive contribution to not just society, but this whole world.

He will not just put money, but also his blood, sweat, tears and guts into the business.

In these times, all we have is casino capitalism run and owned by Wall Street/Dalal Street Pimps.

The only ones who make money in today's Casino Capitalist Stock markets are Wall Street/Dalal Street Pimps, and of course smart investors like me who have figured out the market finally, after being driven even upto bankruptcy by the Wall Street/Dalal Street Pimps.

The biggest con acts in the finance industry today are mutual funds and ULIPs and also so called "strategies" of "Buy and Hold", vigorously promoted by many billionaire investment managers and hedge fund owners.

They want us to "Buy and Hold" so that they can cash their profits.

What the Wall Street/Dalal Street Pimps actually want us to do is not "Buy and Hold" but "Buy and Hold the bag."

So, for now it is better to be a Short term Speculator or an ICU Lottery Ticket Speculator and only risk money you can afford to lose.

With the rest of the money, invest in a property that will get you a residential rental income.

Or invest in a professional company that will invest in residential rental properties.

Or if you are willing to work hard and be hands on to make your investment grow, then invest in a farm and practice progressive and natural chemical free farming which also includes dairy farming.

I hope that by 2026 in Bharat, a farmer with 5-10 acres, who is educated in the art of progressive and natural chemical free farming and cooperative marketing, will be making more money than a software engineer working for an IT/BT Coolie.

Do not invest in any farmland or property now unless you have been lucky enough to already own it.

Wait till 2025 or 2026 to start investing in land and property and also most stocks.

The exemption to investing in stocks even in 2020 applies if you use the formulas for which I have given below which can be invested on when you get the right opportunity to do so.

By 2026 or 2027, prices of land will be 1/10th of today's prices which has led to a bubble in every asset due to the pumping of "free" money by all the FUKUS (France, **UK**, **USA**) central banks and Japan.

I have also given a formula in this publication for investing in stable low risk evergreen dividend paying free cash flow to equity positive stocks trading at a bargain.

Read the Wikipedia article to understand more about free cash flow to equity. The short link is https://bit.ly/3gg57aQ.

Investing in these types of stocks can be done even today since many promising stocks are trading below their book value and still free cash flow to equity positive.

A lot of stocks will end up in the ICU by September 2026.

If you are above 50 and have no debt, put a maximum of 15% of your capital as risk capital, in a basket ICU Lottery ticket stocks again using the formula I give you in this book.

If you are above 60 and have no debt, just use the formula for Low Risk, Stable and Dividend Investing in Evergreen Stocks. If you have money you can afford to lose (mad money), and it will not affect you if you lose it, then put that mad money in a basket of ICU lottery ticket stocks.

If you are below 25 and have no debt, put upto 30% of your capital as risk capital in ICU lottery ticket stocks.

But don't put all your risk capital in one ICU lottery ticket stock, spread it across at least 5 ICU lottery ticket stocks.

Thoroughly study past economic bubbles and crashes for upto 200 years.

Take the Kondratiev Wave seriously.

This calls for even more patience, but if you can follow the Kondratiev Wave, even one trading period of a few months in your life time will change your family for generations.

Knowing when to jump onto the next technological breakthrough and jumping out when you see the end of the cycle can change your family for generations.

Nikolai Kondratiev was one of the most underrated economists, but in my opinion, his theories are most suited in the long term and for this world in general.

He had a lot of significant and useful theories on agriculture, which is the basis and only long-term sustainable policy for any economy.

Unfortunately he was born during Stalin's rule, and Stalin being the asshole that he was, had Nikolai Kondratiev sent to a labour camp and then had him shot for exposing the unpleasant truths of Stalin's policies.

These Kondratiev cycles last as long as 50-60 years.

The tech enabled finance and casino capitalism revolution started in 1971.

I expect it to collapse by March 2026.

All tech and tech enabled finance does is intangible.

All you need is a computer and some smart software to produce profits.

It actually produces nothing, it just drives people and finally countries in to debt, and produces profits only for a few select Wall Street/Dalal Street Pimps and Lalas.

So after mid 2026, the next cycle of the Kondratiev Wave will begin and it will be back to technologies and businesses promoting sustainable growth using tangible and measurable products especially in agriculture, energy (decentralised power grids, Nuclear Fusion and other energy sources from our Shastras and innumerable ancient texts), organic and natural food products and FMCG, traditional healthcare (Ayurveda), artisanal guild cooperative production, community owned banks, water pollution control, water conservation and recharge, biodegradable replacements for plastic and other toxic products, and natural replacements for animal products.

I am setting up an investment fund to chase the above opportunities and have quite a few good leads and potential opportunities.

If you are interested in the above opportunities and are serious and patient and high risk tolerant, then use my feedback form at my company शम्भल समत्वम् (Shambhala Samathvam) to contact me.

Note:

This article was originally written in 2017 and came true in 2020. I have slightly modified it to include today's conditions.

I have slightly modified it to include 2024 conditions as I have revised some sections of the book in October 2024.

My blunders in Speculation

My first investment was in a stock called Hindustan Oil Exploration company (HOEC) with money loaned to me by my father.

This was the days of the early 1990s during the glory days of Harshad Mehta when we had crooked brokers and the market ran only on tips and the madness of ignorant investors like me.

There was no online trading and the only prices were those listed in the Economic Times the next day.

My friend gave me the tip of HOEC. His father's broker had given it to his father.

I did not invest in the MRF IPO in the early 1990s, even though my good friend recommended it to me, because who wanted to invest in a boring tyre company when I could strike gold tomorrow investing in the far more exciting field of oil exploration.

Also why trust a good friend who also happened to be an alcoholic, when you get hot tips from stockbrokers who are supposed to be far more knowledgeable about the stock market than anybody.

I bought HOEC at I think Rs 55/share and within a week the crooked broker told me to sell and he said he sold it at Rs 95/share. I was thrilled.

The next day after the sale, I went to my crooked brokers office, and I saw the closing price was at I think Rs 125/share.

I was upset with my crooked broker. But there was no way to prove at what price he actually sold HOEC, since he said he sold earlier in the day before the price finally closed at Rs 125/share.

This set me on the road to ruin. Looking back, I should have lost money on my first trade.

Then I would not have been so reckless and stupid in the future.

Then in 1997, I went to the USA to do my Master's in Engineering at the University of Florida. I did not start to invest till I got my first job in late 1999.

My father had given me $20000 for my education. I missed the whole dotcom book and kept that money in a savings account earning 0.5% per annum.

In late 1999 when I started earning my own money, I began to short the market. I shorted Amazon and made money during its collapse in 2000.

That further set me on the road to ruin. But I was still very careful of losing money.

Then March 12, 2003, where I my vision of the prophecy of the advent of the Satyuga happened and due to the wonders of the Baker Act I was introduced to the horrors of Zyprexa.

Just before the Zyprexa was forcibly introduced to me I came across a golden opportunity in Healthsouth.

It had fallen to a lifetime low of 30 cents a share and I bought $13,000 worth of shares. Healthsouth was expected to go bankrupt but I did a thorough analysis and knew it would come through.

Healthsouth did not go bankrupt and within 18 months my Healthsouth investment was worth $400,000. I took out this money and put it all of it into Calpine (before it went bankrupt) which had fallen to an all-time low.

Calpine suddenly shot up and within a day I had made $100,000. So I had more than $590,000 in early 2006.

By this time the Zyprexa had completely raped my mind and body, but I felt like the God of the stock market.

I hated to borrow money, I had never borrowed a single dollar in my life before I was forcibly introduced to Zyprexa due to the wonders of the Baker Act .

After I got addicted to Zyprexa, I started to borrow great amounts of money and also gamble in options, the most risky form of trading in the stock market.

I started to gamble in options because I wanted to make money the fastest possible way to buy out my father's share in his company, since he told me if I gave him the money, he put into the company he would let me run it.

Looking back that was the second most foolish decision I made in my life.

I also got involved with a girl who I met on the internet and who I would not have even glanced at if I were in my normal senses.

I got involved with her because an Internet website matched us up saying that we were perfectly compatible and we both were fans of Mr Spock of Star Trek .

In fact, in 2006, I put my entire life's savings (around $500,000) and even borrowed $100,000 from my credit cards, for a total of $590,000 and put it all on options and I lost all of it.

Looking back in 2024 at what happened in 2006, I laugh at it as a tragi-comedy.

I did not lose $590,000 in a single put, I lost $216,000 in a single put.

But overall I lost $590,000 in just 3 months gambling in options because I was forcibly put on Zyprexa due to the wonders of the Baker Act in Florida, and this seriously impaired my judgement and sense of risk.

In May 2006, I had gambled $216,000 on LNG puts and was underwater by $200,000 by June 2006.

I still had hope till expiry day in June 2006, but unfortunately on expiry day I had an entanglement with an alcoholic loser girlfriend who did not understand the stock market.

I was in a 5-star hotel in Goa, India at the time and it was 8pm in the evening, just past 930am opening time in USA.

I saw the LNG puts go up and wanted to stay awake the whole night till 2am in India which would be closing time in the USA.

The LNG puts started to pick up volume and I knew I would recover my fortune.

My loser girlfriend had drunk 8 beers from the hotel minibar ($$$) and was drunk and screaming for me to sell in our hotel room and in panic I sold just to calm her down and went to bed with just a $15,000 gain for the day.

But I was underwater $185,000 out of which $100,000 was borrowed from my credit cards.

The sad part is that the next morning when I woke up, if I held on to those puts till closing, I would have recovered all my losses and made over $150,000.

That was the lowest point in my life in financial speculation and it was all God's plan to teach me about Karma.

I and the alcoholic loser split up soon after that.

Only my dad's intervention and valuable bailout funding saved me from bankruptcy.

I returned to Bharat for good in 2009 and started to speculate in the Bharatiya stock market. Based on my success in the USA, I only looked for beaten down stocks.

In 2011, I saw Arvind Mills at around Rs 28, but preferred to buy Surya Pharma at 30 paisa. Surya Pharma went bankrupt and Arvind Mills went to Rs 300 by 2017.

In 2014, I got Rs 80,00,000 as my gratuity from my old company and also a gift from my father. I was still following my USA success model of buying beaten down stocks.

I put all of it on a fraud stock Rasoya Proteins. I was really stupid, during the same time I also identified Tanla Solutions, Morepen Labs, Confidence Petroleum, Mawana Sugars and Ludlow Jute, but instead of diversifying my bets, I got greedy and put it all on the single fraud stock called Rasoya Proteins because it was the cheapest of all my picks and also more importantly it was trading at sub rupee values and Money Control and also Rasoya latest financial years auditor's reports also said its book value was Rs 7.

Fortunately, I learnt the from the bitter USA experience of borrowing and investing and never borrowed to invest in this stupid bet on Rasoya Proteins. Unfortunately, I also advised my good friend to do the same and both of us lost all our money.

I should have spread my bets across Rasoya and the other stocks that I had identified.

I also started gambling in options because I made Rs 8,00,000 in one day in 2015.

By early 2018 I had lost all my money.

But the good thing was I had started practicing ध्यान (Dhyana) or what is loosely translated as meditation in 2015.

By late 2018 I was completely drug free. I started to think again just like I used to in 2000. I had a sense of risk and discipline again.

But this time in mid-2018, I went back and looked at all my major trades both in the USA and Bharat right from the days I started investing in the early 1990s.

That is where I saw the mistakes that I had made by not investing in MRF, Amazon and Apple even though the opportunities to do so came and bit me in the face. That is where I saw the foolishness of my gambling in futures and options. That is where I saw to foolishness of putting all my capital in a single trade.

I have learned the end result is that its always better to buy and hold than gamble in futures and options and short-term trading.

AAPL was trading at $8 in 2006. It is now $364 as of July 1, 2020.

My $590,000 in 2006, would have become around 27 million in 2020 if I just bought AAPL instead of gambling in options way back in 2006.

Oh well that's the follies of youth - falling for quick thrills and excitement instead of safety and stability.

The foolishness of falling for the excitement of oil exploration instead of choosing the boring stability of boring tyre companies.

I would like to think I am older and wiser now. Only time will tell, but my results since early 2019 upto July 1, 2020 have been very encouraging.

In early 2018 I started investing in gold ETFs. I knew the market was going to tank and knew that gold was the safest investment. My bet proved right and as of June 2020, I have returned more than 50% on my investment in gold ETFs.

Over the last 5 years from FY 20-21, as you can see from the below image taken from my Portfolio Updates link, I have probably achieved a world record, forget India record in investing in any financial market in the world with in XIRR of 83% as of August 9, 2024 from FY 20-21.

Now in investing and in any financial investment or business I get into now, I look for safety, stability, and a return more than inflation. I no longer try to double my money in a week.

For excitement I do ध्यान (Dhyana) and when I get a chance to do skydiving again I will do that also for excitement.

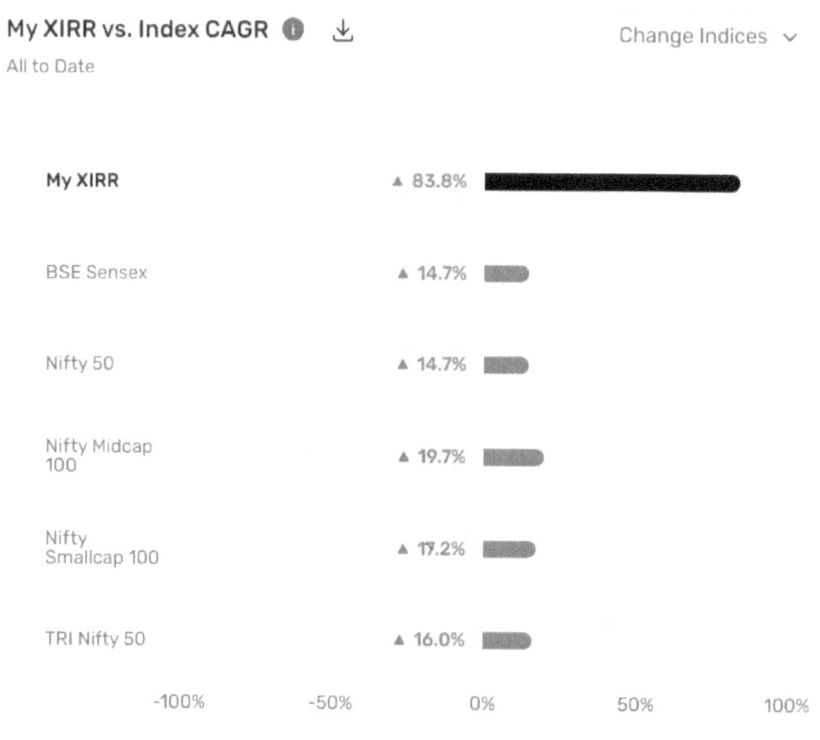

5 Year XIRR from FY 20-21 to August 9, 2024

My life's learning in Speculation

I was fascinated by the stock market ever since Harshad Mehta became famous.

People have mixed views about Harshad Mehta, but if it wasn't for him, many people including me would have not been fascinated by the stock market.

It was not the thousands of crores, his Lexus cars or his penthouse with a mini golf course that really made him important.

That was only to fill and sell the magazines and TV shows.

More importantly it was the mass hysteria that he created which made him extremely powerful.

Just rumours of his investment took a junk stock like Karnataka Ball Bearings to more than 100 times it original value in a few months.

If rumours of his selling a stock came, that stock collapsed.

Banks were lining up and running behind him to give him money to invest.

It was not the money that he made or the fancy stuff that he had, but the power that he had over the Bharatiya stock market is what fascinated me.

The power that Harshad Mehta had and the madness he inspired is what led to my introduction to speculating in the financial markets.

I am largely a self-taught speculator.

After more than 31 years of speculation, and big wins and even bigger losses I thought I should at least briefly write down my lessons from my experience so that people can learn from both my mistakes and successes.

One can never truly be a master at speculation. It is a continuous learning processes and every trade is a new lesson to be learnt.

Speculation is a combination of both art and science.

It is very rare to find a person who has a combination of both artistic and scientific talents.

But such people who can combine both artistic and scientific abilities make the best speculators.

In fact, not just in speculation, but in any field, the people who combine both art and science into their work, will come out as the highest winners in their field.

To be a success in speculation you must conquer four fundamental things:

- Ignorance
- Fear
- Hope
- Greed

To eliminate ignorance:

- Follow overall market patterns for at least 18 months to two years

- Focus on trading and delivery volumes, not just daily, but more importantly weekly and monthly volumes.
- Focus on the charts and institutional buying and selling, and insider buying and selling
- Focus on pledging of shares

Using the above guidelines, you will gain some measure of knowledge.

Ignore and black out all the news, especially TV news and internet message boards.

Remember the stock market is only 15-20% of the financial markets.

There are much larger and profitable and less manipulated markets like commodities, bonds and currencies which also offer immense opportunities.

These markets are still manipulated, but unlike investing in the stock market which is completely opaque, the commodities and currency markets are relatively more transparent.

However, the commodities, bonds and currencies markets are usually derivative based and hence it is not advisable to put more than 2% of your total capital in any derivative instrument.

In Bharat, only the equities markets are developed and extremely liquid, so trading in the commodities and currency markets in Bharat has huge spreads and low liquidity.

Trading in the bond markets is only available to professionals and is the most opaque and illiquid market.

All the markets in the world are tied to the USA.

If the USA markets fall, the whole world falls. If the USA markets rise the whole world rises.

So for the best trends in the USA for equities, financials and commodities follow the CBOE Commitments of Traders (CBOE COT).

The CBOE Commitments of Traders (CBOE COT) is the best indicator for the trend of the market.

Here is an explanation of the CBOE COT – https://bit.ly/2NQNzpH.

However the CBOE COT is only numbers and very difficult to understand.

As they say a picture speaks a thousand words, so to look at the CBOE COT in pictures, use the CME Quik Strike.

This gives you the map of the USA markets.

With this map if you learn to navigate it properly you will have at least a 20% idea of the trend.

The rest is left to chance since the markets are completely irrational.

It is run on the madness of crowds and as we know madness can never be understood.

Genius is found even in madness but is limited to probably one in a million.

For the rest of the crowd all that is found is madness.

That all the secrets I reveal about my practices.

You figure out who to follow from CME Quik Strike.

Another good site is the Barchart.com Commitments of Traders.

These charts are much easier and simpler to read than the CME Quik Strike and give the added advantage of the current price of the commodity also.

Hint:

The Managed Money are the wolves.

The Dealers are the shepherds and the Producers are the sheep – they can fight the wolves and direct the sheep.

Shepherds can even direct the sheep off the cliff and the sheep will blindly jump.

But sometimes the sheep just jump over the fence and run away and escape and leave the shepherd and wolves chasing after them.

The most exciting market in the world is the Shanghai Composite (SSEC).

The Shanghai Composite (SSEC) is a good gamblers most orgasmic wet dream and a clueless gamblers worst nightmare.

The Shanghai Composite (SSEC) can fall 4% in a day and rise 2% the next day.

Can you imagine the scale and magnitude of profits or losses that can be made by trading on the Shanghai Composite (SSEC)?

However, do not speculate in the F&O, commodities and currency markets with **not more than 0.5% of your net liquid capital (net cash only**, **not counting your investments** in land, gold, bluechip and good stocks etc), after all expenses, including your planned foreign world tour with your wife, mistress or toy boy whichever may be the case.

I have made huge amounts of money before I reached 30, that ordinary people would not make in a lifetime.

But finally, I have only been an eventual failure in speculation over the last 25 years until early 2018.

That is because I could not conquer hope and greed.

People may conquer fear but hope and greed is the is downfall of most speculators.

Forget about candlesticks, momentum, MACD, CCI and fundamental analysis.

No matter how many books you read, or however many years of experience you have, if you cannot conquer fear, hope, and greed, you will never be a success in speculation.

First develop a disciplined mind to conquer fear, but more importantly to conquer hope and greed.

The only way to conquer fear, hope and greed is by the sincere and sustained practice of ध्यान (Dhyan closely translated as Meditation) to achieve समत्वम् (Samathvam or Equanimity).

Of course I must not forget to mention that before you start to practice ध्यान (Dhyan) in speculation, it always helps to get kicked in the face many times so that you feel and understand what fear, hope and greed is.

Only when you feel and understand fear, hope, and greed, then you have some chance of learning to conquer it.

You cannot do this by paper trading, you must put your real money at risk.

Of course, since you are putting real money at risk, only put money that you can afford to lose.

Of course, you can be a bigger ass like me and make and then piss away huge amounts of money so that you learn what real fear, hope, and greed is.

But what I did was totally unnecessary, and I would not advise anybody to make my mistakes.

In the recent past from 2019 onwards, I have learnt to conquer hope, but more importantly I am learning to conquer greed.

So, my results are starting to improve since 2019.

I have returned more than 50% on my investments from late 2018 to date as of June 2020 when markets the world over have negative returns.

Over the last 5 years from FY 20-21, as you can see from my Portfolio Updates link, I have probably achieved a world record, forget India record in investing in any financial market in the world with in XIRR of 83% as of August 9, 2024 from FY 20-21.

I am ordinarily not a greedy person at all.

Almost all the money I have I spend on others.

Ask my friends what I would do if I had only Rs 10 in my pocket and saw someone in need.

But when I speculate, I used to get very greedy.

I wanted double the profits than what I already had.

I would double my bets instead of taking my cards off the table.

This has been my downfall till the recent past until early 2018.

I figure if even a world class speculator like Jesse Livermore did break his rules and make mistakes, I also have made the same mistakes, but hopefully am learning not to repeat them in the future.

Jesse Livermore broke his rules so often that he finally went bankrupt and shot his brains out.

That happens when you don't learn from getting kicked in the face many times.

Learning the Art of Investing

The bible of all value investors is Benjamin Graham's The Intelligent Investor.

One of the best teachers in India of investing in the stock market is Vishal Khandelwal of Safal Niveshak (Hindi term for 'successful investor').

Vishal also has a very enlightening Youtube Channel where he interviews some of the world's leading investors and investment writers and experts.

To learn the basic terms of Investing Analysis and Stock Research Analysis I would strongly recommend Research Analyst By National Institute of Securities Markets | An Educational Initiative of SEBI.

For today's more tech savvy generation there is **Zerodha Varsity** (https://zerodha.com/varsity/)

For those who want a professional IIT Level course for free, check out my youtube listing NPTEL Security Analysis & Portfolio Management by Prof JP Singh, Dept of Management Studies, IIT Roorkee.

Stock Analysis and Valuation Sites

Value Research (https://www.valueresearchonline.com/) — India's best independent stock analysis and research website. No app is available.

Trendlyne (https://trendlyne.com/) — Among India's best valuation site with loads of information for all Indian stocks. An App is available at Rs 4000/year and free limited version also is available.

Smart Investing (https://www.smart-investing.in/) – No app – Rs 3000/year — very good traditional valuation site but only for stocks above 100 crore market cap.

Simply Wall.st – Good valuation site based on DCF valuation — can track all stocks in the world App is there $200/year and free limited version also is available.

For trading Analysis and Volumes and Price Action Stock Edge (https://www.stockedge.com/) – very good stock analysis site for deliveries and technical scans and also for fundamental information and India's best trading analysis site. App is there Rs 4000/year and free limited version also is available.

Webull (https://www.webull.com/) – A free and most helpful app to view real time money flow and trading action and price action, can trade all stocks in the world, worlds best real time trading analysis site and best of all it is completely free. Has currently stopped data flow and money flow for Indian stock markets.

The Mindset and Psychology of Speculation

My favourite all time book on speculation is Reminiscences of a Stock Operator.

It is about Jesse Livermore, the greatest speculator in modern history.

By the age of 15, he earned $1000 ($28000, Rs 18,00,000 in 2017 value).

He made $100,000,000 ($1.4 billion, Rs 9100 crores in 2017 value) in the crash of 1929.

Just follow the below rules by Jesse Livermore and you will be a success at speculation:

1.Cut your losses.

2. Let your winners run.

3. Nothing new ever occurs in the business of speculating or investing in securities and commodities.

4. Money cannot consistently be made trading every day or every week during the year.

5. Don't trust your own opinion and back your judgment until the action of the market itself confirms your opinion.

6. Markets are never wrong - opinions often are.

7. The real money made in speculating has been in commitments showing in profit right from the start.

8. As long as a stock is acting right, and the market is right, do not be in a hurry to take profits.

9. One should never permit speculative ventures to run into investments.

10. The money lost by speculation alone is small compared with the gigantic sums lost by so-called investors who have let their investments ride.

11. Never buy a stock because it has had a big decline from its previous high.

12. Never sell a stock because it seems high-priced.

13. I become a buyer as soon as a stock makes a new high on its movement after having had a normal reaction.

14. Never average losses.

15. *The human side of every person is the greatest enemy of the average investor or speculator.*

16. *Wishful thinking must be banished.*

17. *Big movements take time to develop.*

18. *It is not good to be too curious about all the reasons behind price movements.*

19. *It is much easier to watch a few than many.*

20. *If you cannot make money out of the leading active issues, you are not going to make money out of the stock market as a whole.*

21. *The leaders of today may not be the leaders of two years from now.*

22. *Do not become completely bearish or bullish on the whole market because one stock in some particular group has plainly reversed its course from the general trend.*

23. *Few people ever make money on tips. Beware of inside information. If there was easy money lying around, no one would be forcing it into your pocket.*

There was one very important lesson that Jesse Livermore forgot to mention.

Never put all your eggs in one basket.

Never go for "All or Nothing", because most times you will end up with nothing.

This does not just apply to investing, but to any aspect of your life.

Never risk more than 15% of your trading capital in a single long-term equity trade.

If you are trading short term and volatile products, never put more than 2% of your trading capital in a single trade.

Always use limit orders when you buy and sell, never use market orders.

Do not set automatic stop orders unless you cannot watch the market regularly. If you cannot watch the market regularly then set automatic stop orders below set moving averages chosen on the volatility of the stock.

The follies of "Investing" In Real Estate

Real Estate is the most overrated "investment" as of 2024 especially in developing countries like Bharat.

The Everything Bubble has burst in 2020, just like the bubble of 2008, preceded by the dotcom bubble of 2000.

I have watched the real estate bubble burst in the USA in 2008.

I was physically present in the USA and almost got sucked into following the mania of that time according to the book Rich Dad Poor Dad by that famous useful idiot Robert Kiyosaki.

Properties that were running at $200,000 in 2006 could not find buyers at $50,000 in 2009.

Due to the pumping of "free" money by the FUKUS central banks and rest of the central banks of the developed world, the property values in the USA and other developed markets were reinflated until 2020.

The real estate market in Bharat has been a real estate speculators most orgasmic wet dream from the mid-1980s up to 2020. It has only seen an upside.

Bharat is the most overvalued real estate market in the world.

Bharat has not seen the bubble burst completely as of yet. What has happened until June 2024, is not even a side show.

Extract from article: House Prices/GDP per Capita in Bharat compared to Asia (https://bit.ly/2Zyn2D7)

House Prices/GDP per Capita in India compared to Asia

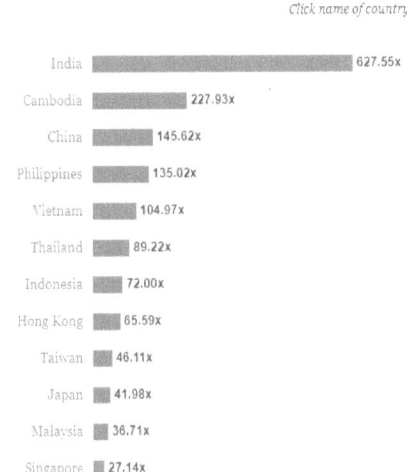

Footnote | Export

Sort: Alphabetically | Ascending Rank | Descending Rank
Click name of country for detailed information

Country	Value
India	627.55x
Cambodia	227.93x
China	145.62x
Philippines	135.02x
Vietnam	104.97x
Thailand	89.22x
Indonesia	72.00x
Hong Kong	65.59x
Taiwan	46.11x
Japan	41.98x
Malaysia	36.71x
Singapore	27.14x

■ **India: House price to income ratio**

The house price to income ratio is the ratio of the cost of a typical upscale housing unit of 100 square metres, compared to the countrys GDP per capita. Normally this ratio will be much higher in low income countries than in high income countries.

Just to give you an idea of how overvalued the Bharatiya market has become, read the live case study below.

In the mid 1970s, my father was a mid-level military officer deputed to the Survey of India.

I think I remember him telling me his monthly salary was Rs 3000.

A Sovereign of gold (8gm) was Rs 165.

A Premier Padmini car was Rs 18,000 worth around five 60 x40 sites (2400 sqft sites) in an upcoming locality like Indiranagar.

So, by today's equivalent my father was earning 18 Sovereigns of gold per month which is an extremely high salary in Bharat.

In the late 1970s, the plot we are currently staying in, which was adjacent to my grandfather's house was sold for Rs 29000 (about 175 Sovereigns of gold).

Despite their high salaries, my father and mother were unable to come up with the money to purchase this plot even as far as the late 1970s.

Today the plot we are staying in is valued at Rs 3,60,00,000. Just the plot, it does not include the house.

That is equivalent to 1071 Sovereigns of gold.

And gold is at the highest it has ever been in history, as of June 2020.

A highly paid person like my father earning 18 Sovereigns of gold per month could not afford it at 175 sovereigns of gold even in the 1970s.

Which person earns 1071 Sovereigns of gold a year today in Bharat or anywhere in the world?

Only crooked politicians, bureaucrats and Wall Street/Dalal Street Pimps and Lalas.

Their day of reckoning has come. All the real estate projects and real estate firms they invested their black money in will go bankrupt.

Real estate projects will be abandoned or sold like Lehman Brothers at hugely distressed rates.

Rental yields are less than 2% of investment value. You get more yield in a USA CD.

Net income from agricultural land, even the most high cash crop producing agricultural land in places like Kodagu is at an income to value ratio of 55.

That means to earn a net profit of Rs 75,000/acre in a highly profitable zone like Kodagu you need to invest Rs 25,00,000 for an acre of land.

This works out to a net yield of 3% on investment value. You get more yield in a German CD.

And Kodagu is the richest and highest tax paying district in Karnataka after Bangalore and probably one of the richest agricultural districts in the whole of Bharat.

So, you can imagine how overvalued agricultural land also is in the whole of Bharat.

Land is only headed downwards for the next 10 years especially in Bharat, where, as of July 2020, House Prices/GDP ratio in Bharat is 627, far more than even Singapore which has a house price of House Prices/GDP of 27.

Singapore itself is an overvalued market even at a House Prices/GDP of 27.

I have seriously studied housing bubbles, and historically in any market where the house price is more than 3 times a person's annual income, that real estate market is overvalued.

Look at your annual income and the prices of houses in your area. Look at the rental yield on those houses in your area.

Imagine how far real estate is going to fall all over the world especially in a hugely overvalued market like Bharat.

I am sure this applies to many places all over the world especially black money recyclers and tax havens like New York, London, Geneva, and Dubai.

I would not be surprised if the real estate market returned to at least its historical ratio in the 1970s of 175 Sovereigns of gold for an 1800 sqft plot in a premium area of Bangalore.

That means an 1800 sqft plot in a premium area of Bangalore will cost around Rs 60,00,000 compared to today's value of Rs 3,60,00,000.

I know this sounds insane, but remember the same thing happened in the USA during the crash of 2008.

A lot of high income people earn Rs 20,00,000 per year in Bangalore, so this will return to its historical mean of 3 times a person's annual income.

This is for a high income area, so you can imagine what the prices will fall to in low income areas which form the vast majority of Bangalore and also Bharat.

I expect this to happen by 2026.

Most people speculate in real estate in hope of appreciation. What happens when it tanks like I have predicted?

Land is a finite asset. There must be strict rules on speculation of land.

Holding land for speculation must be made an awfully expensive proposition that people think twice before speculation on land.

We should have a urban land ceiling and only exempt urban land accumulation if urban land is accumulated at a single location by individuals for themselves and their children, and not by corporates.

After all you cannot be physically present in two locations and individuals cannot have access to millions and billions of dollars like corporates.

I don't think we should have a land ceiling on land used for agricultural or plantation purposes or land used for environmental conservation or projects of social and charitable benefits for the construction and running of the सत् देवालय Sat Devalaya (True Temples).

However, we should regularly verify at least on a bi-annual basis, that land purchased for such purposes is actually being put to this use otherwise we should confiscate this excess land that was fraudulently purchased.

Land used for agricultural or plantation purposes should only be allowed to be accumulated by individual families or family owned farming companies or Cooperative Farmer Producer Organisations (FPOS), upto 2000 acres and first preference should only be given to locals who reside in the area or who have roots in the area or plan to purchase the land and move physically and established that newly purchase land as their primary residence.

Land used for environmental conservation or projects of social and charitable benefits should only be restricted to charitable societies and non-profit organisations.

However, this exemption should not include educational institutions with so called "non-profit" status which is the biggest scam in India after "non-profit" Health and Religious Institutions which are equally big scams.

This sort of verification of land purchased for agricultural, plantation and environmental conservation, can easily be done on a completely automated basis by machine learning and remote sensing, even on a weekly time period, with absolutely no human interference, at a very low cost compared to actually sending out humans to do this job.

As far as possible this verification process should remove human influence since it could lead to malpractices.

A few times, people accumulate such land for their families or because they want to do agriculture, forest or environment conservation or projects of social and charitable benefits for the construction and running of the सत् देवालय Sat Devalaya (True Temples).

I think these are the only kinds of people who should be allowed to get away with accumulating land.

For the rest of the real estate speculators, especially Representative DFIs, corrupt Sarkari babus, and Wall Street/Dalal Street Pimps and Lalas, holding land should be made an extremely expensive proposition that they will not even attempt to purchase land unless they intend to put it to a fair and reasonable use.

Short Term Trading

This form of trading covers hourly to daily to weekly to monthly and applies to currencies but can also be applied to other short-term instruments like commodity and equity and futures and options.

As far as possible never speculate in equity and equity index futures and options. It is just a waste of time, money, and resources.

Only writers of these options consistently make money. Options buyers lose money 999 times out of 1000.

Never write options with your own hard earned money, this is only done by people who are using OPM (Other People's Money) and people using OPM are only found among the Wall Street/Dalal Street Pimps.

For short term trading the only person I would recommend to learn from is Chris Lee from Pip Mavens (https://www.pipmavens.com/).

He has taken 11 years and lost more than $ 350,000 before he became a profitable trader so if you learn from him you will save 11 years and probably not have to lose more than $10000 after you master his instructions.

Chris Lee writes like Zen Master, and his trading is also like a Zen Master, at least from the equity curve what he shows on his website which I assume to be the truth and needs to be verified from his trade log which I dont have access to and I cannot validate his claims and screenshots and take no responsibility for his claims on his website.

Long Term Trading

This form of trading covers a period 1 to 5 years or more even upto 10 years.

High Risk Investing – The Art of ICU Lottery Ticket Speculation

Due to dumb luck, or maybe some talent, I am not sure which, I have been a reasonable success at ICU Lottery Ticket Speculation.

ICU Lottery Ticket Speculation means investing in almost dead stocks or stocks which have fallen significantly from their highs.

They were once flourishing companies, but due to some turn of fortune and change in business conditions they ended up in the ICU.

Just like for a human, there are only two outcomes for a stock in the ICU:

Death or Recovery.

This is a risky and extremely complicated method of speculation.

The odds of success even among the most sophisticated of ICU Lottery Ticket speculators is less than 15%.

But if even one of that 15% clicks, you can make more than 10+ times your money when the stock recovers.

My success rate in ICU Lottery Ticket Speculation has been more than 40% in the USA, and more than 60% in India.

I have only one ICU Lottery Ticket now.

In the biggest Wall Street Pimp whose collapse caused worldwide turmoil in 2008 – Lehman Brothers.

Hopefully, it should pay off by late 2024 and even if it goes bust, I have learned my lessons from my previous mistakes and have only invested money I can afford to lose.

As a rule, never invest in stocks that have already declared bankruptcy. Most likely 99 times out of hundred, they will be declared worthless and cancelled or diluted to infinity.

Invest in stocks which are in the ICU – they are not bankrupt yet and there is a possibility of recovery. If stocks declare bankruptcy that means they are already dead.

My Principles of ICU Lottery Ticket Speculation

- The first principle of ICU Lottery Ticket Speculation is extreme patience.

It sometimes takes as much as two years to see at least 2X returns and in the meanwhile the stock could at the worst decline by 60% or even 80% and at the best could remain flat and go nowhere.

In those two years you probably would have made more money in a USA savings account (it is only 0.5% interest in the USA compared to 4% in any Bharatiya savings account).

Some of you may think that if a stock declines by 60% it is going to fail.

There are conditions to this decline.

If it is a sudden fall on huge volume, then better to get out.

But if it is a gradual fall on very low volume, then this is the best time to accumulate in 45 – 70 day intervals.

Start to accumulate only when the trend has flattened out or begins to turn upwards. Never accumulate in a downward trend or falling knife.

To spot a trend change in the stock follow the money flow in the Webull app for at least two months.

Webull is doing a valuable service to humanity by providing such valuable information for free in its extremely useful app.

Volumes in such stocks are extremely low and illiquid so that is why I say only risk money you can afford to lose.

Some of you may think that you can keep your money in a savings account and then invest just before the stock is going to go up.

This is a very difficult thing to do and can only be done if you have insider knowledge and it is illegal to trade based on insider knowledge.

Martha Stewart who was almost a billionaire, sold a stock when informed by an insider, to avoid a loss of less than $50,000.

This cost her 6 months in jail and a 2-year house arrest.

Same was the case with Rajat Gupta.

He never even made a penny from the insider information he leaked, but it cost him two years in the big house.

This sort of punishment is very rare in Bharat.

Here, even a world class fraud POS like the King of Good Times still remains a member of Parliament, walks free and probably will still be left with his overseas holdings which are enough for his generations.

- The second principle of ICU Lottery Ticket Speculation is that you must be prepared to lose money but cut your losses by strictly setting a limit on how much you can lose and sell at all costs when you lose more than the limit you set.

Never hope it will go back up, just sell if your limits are broken.

If it starts to go back up, then buy it again after it starts going back up.

Also set sliding limits as you make profits. As your investment moves up, raise the sell limit so that what little profit you make is banked if the investment falls below your limit. Keep raising your sell price limit as the investment goes up.

Do not at any cost maintain your sell limit at your original buying price. Bank whatever profit you get if your sliding sell limit is broken.

- The third principle of ICU Lottery Ticket Speculation is that you must let your profits run.

If you follow the above principal of sliding limits you should have a good chance of letting your profits run.

- The fourth principle of ICU Lottery Ticket Speculation is that you should not put more than 10% or a maximum of 15% of your capital in any single stock and in that you should cut your losses if the stock declines by more than 15%.

- The fifth principle and this is most important is to figure out which stock is down due to bad business strategy and which stock is down due to the dubious morals of the management.

I lost a good bit of money because I was not familiar with the morals of the management of the companies listed in the stock market in Bharat.

But in the USA, my strike rate was more than 50%, some of the huge wins I made was Healthsouth and Calpine (before it went bankrupt). Incidentally Lehman Brothers shorted Calpine into bankruptcy.

In the USA most stocks go bankrupt because of high debt and aggressive expansion and also because of shady and dubious morals of the professional management who have no stake in the company and leave all the risk to the shareholders in pursuit of their bonuses and stock options.

In Bharat most stocks mainly go bankrupt because of the shady and dubious morals of the management and promoters of these companies.

They are most willing to milk the company dry to enhance their personal fortunes.

- The sixth principle is that the most exciting time to invest in an ICU lottery ticket stock is when it is doing nothing for at least 8-12 months and has crossed it all time low over at least 8-12 months. So, you must watch these stocks for a long time.

- The seventh principle is to never catch a falling knife. It is only very rarely that stocks that have fallen sharply bounce back in a fast time. Most of the stocks that fall sharply either go bankrupt or reach their all-time lows in about 12-18 months after beginning of the collapse of the stock.

- The eight principle is to keep your powder dry. Do not invest just for the sake of investing or because you have money to invest. Wait for the right opportunity. Always keep your investing money liquid in a liquid daily dividend fund which you can deploy in two or three days. Do not keep it in a bank deposit. Liquid daily dividend funds give more returns and since they are dividends, they are tax free.

- The ninth principle is do not jump blindly into the pool. First dip your toes into it and use the steps to descend into the pool. Never invest all at once in a stock. Always do so in instalments, may be a week, month or even six months depending on the volatility of a stock. The more volatile the stock is, then take even more time of at least 2-3 months between each investment. Do not make short term investments in volatile stocks unless you are prepared to watch them and trade them frequently in a daily basis.

- Little drops of water make the ocean. Forget about huge 1000% gains in a one-time big investment. Instead invest in little drops to make a good ocean which rises and fills slowly with every drop.

But remember oceans once formed, lift all boats, and even destroy not only boats, but entire cities if there is too much tide. So, learn to ride the oceans, and always float above the tides.

The moment the tide gets too rough, get off the boat (liquidate your investment) and head to safe dry land (keep the money in liquid daily dividend funds till the next opportunity comes up.)

- Thoroughly study past economic bubbles and crashes for upto 300 years.

- Take the Kondratiev Wave seriously. This calls for even more patience, but if you can follow the Kondratiev Wave, even one trading period of a few months in your lifetime will change your family for generations.

Knowing when to jump onto the next technological breakthrough and jumping out when you see the end of the cycle can change your family for generations.

- And finally, the last and most important principle of ICU lottery ticket speculation:

Find a regular job, work hard and smart and with devotion and learn from your job experience and then start a business in what you are good at and invest most of your money in what you are good at.

Even in what you are good at do not invest more than 15-20% of your net worth.

- Just use money you can afford to lose in ICU lottery ticket speculation.

That is what you do if you are a sensible lottery player, you only gamble what you can afford to lose.

Do not mortgage your grandfather's house and wife's jewellery to do ICU lottery ticket speculation, because there is a very good chance you will no longer have the winning ICU lottery tickets, grandfather's house and even your wife.

The Art of Low Risk, Stable and Dividend Investing in Evergreen Stocks

This is one of the best articles I have come across on HNI Investing and the mistakes we are making following conventional myths.

Most damaging myths in Indian investing: Perils of an Indian HNI (https://bit.ly/2VDkoux)

More importantly he has given the formula to identify good investments.

Extract from the above article:

How to compound with relatively low risk.

No one that we have met can time the stock market. Neither can we, and we make no attempt to do so. We know of only one way to generate significant real returns in a consistent manner - buy clean, well-managed Bharatiya companies selling essential products behind very high barriers to entry. We call it the Consistent Compounding approach, and have seen it work, both in theory and in practice.

To build the portfolio without using any human judgement each year on June 30 we invest in stocks which in each of the preceding 10 years have grown revenues in double digits and delivered pre-tax-ROCE of at least 15% per annum (throughout the 10-year period). Then hold these stocks for the next 10 years. If you had invested Rs 100 using this method on

June 30, 2000 then in mid-May 2020 your wealth would have compounded to Rs 1,463, a compounded return of 14.4 per cent per annum.

In contrast, the same exercise with the Sensex would have yielded Rs 673 implying a return of 10.1 per cent per annum (both expressed on a total return basis.) In short, in the space of 20 years, using the most rudimentary of financial filters, this method of investing would give almost 15 times compounding as opposed to a mere 7 times compounding from Sensex.

My formula for Low Risk High Income Investing

Invest in consistently dividend paying stocks that have paid at least 8% annual dividend (on current market price) over the last 5 years and are quoting at a discount to current audited book value and are generating positive free cash flow to equity.

If free cash flow to equity has come down, but it is still generating positive operating cash flow, then that also can be considered.

I have arrived at my formula after trying various alternatives over the last 26 years and losing money and now finally making money using this formula.

My immense opportunity loss in MRF is living proof of the virtues of this method.

My formula applies to the Bharatiya stock market.

In Western markets anything with a 3–4% dividend yield is equivalent to a Bharatiya stock paying an 8% dividend yield.

You miss the forest for the trees if you speculate in equity futures and options and do short term trading.

Instead have a longer-term view of at least 10 years.

I probably was one of those rare people who made money shorting Amazon in the dot com collapse of 2000.

But if I had a long term vision, I would have invested Amazon for at least 30 years during the dot com collapse of 2000 and made many multiples of the amount I made with my short term vision of shorting Amazon in 2000.

This painful opportunity loss of not investing in Amazon in the dot com collapse of 2000 has now made me abandon shorting, and equity futures and equity options and have a long term vision of at least 5 years, if not 15 years for promising and fundamentally sound stocks.

To make you feel even worse, if I had only invested the money my father loaned to me in the early 1990s in a first investment of MRF Tyres IPO which was recommended to me by a good knowledgeable friend, instead of trying to make a fast buck on a tip of HOEC from my other speculator like me friend, I would have had more than Rs 500 crores by now, more money than my father ever made in his extremely successful business.

MRF Tyres IPO came out at Rs 10 in the early 1990s. MRF Tyres is Rs 65800 as of June 29, 2020 and gave a dividend of Rs 540/share in 2019.

I did not invest in the MRF IPO in the early 1990s, even though my good friend recommended it to me, because who wanted to invest in a boring tyre company when I could strike gold tomorrow investing in the far more exciting field of oil exploration.

Also why trust a good friend, when you get hot tips from stockbrokers who are supposed to be far more knowledgeable about the stock market than anybody.

Extract from article Rs 11 to Rs 54,000 in 26 years! This stock made patient investors crorepati (https://bit.ly/31EZ5MN)

On April 27, 1993, the company's share closed at Rs 11 compared to the current price of Rs 54,488 on BSE. The scrip hit its lifetime high of Rs 81,423 on April 30, 2018.

My mistakes and more importantly the lessons I have learnt should give you a good lesson on the follies of speculating in futures and options, short term investing, hot tips from crooked stockbrokers, and foolishly choosing exciting instead of boring.

Instead now have the wisdom I now have of focussing on and learning the virtues of long term positive free cash flow to equity investing.

Both in Bharat and the USA, March and April of 2020 was a very good time to buy such consistently dividend paying stocks with positive free cash flow to equity since they were trading at multiyear lows and below book value.

The overall stock markets have run up significantly from March and will fall below their March lows by the end of this year 2020.

It will again be a good time to pick up such consistently dividend paying stocks with positive free cash flow stocks after November 2020.

Above is just my opinion and I could be wrong.

One can only make calculated guesses with proper risk management, the stock market is completely unpredictable.

The most evergreen sector to invest in is the power sector. This includes power generation, power distribution and sectors that deal with power solutions.

Of all the types of power generation, hydro power is most appealing since it has a high moat of entry into this sector and currently is the lowest cost of power generation and will remain so for the next 10 years.

Do not invest in solar energy, wind energy and the "Enron on wheels" firms like Tesla promoting battery operated e-vehicles.

They are on the road to obsolescence and most solar and wind projects in Bharat are just to recycle black money into white.

The power sector is known as the *"Widows and Orphans"* sector for the last 100 years because it is the only reliable source of income for people like widows and orphans.

Please note the above comments of mine has my vision window of only 10 years (upto 2030).

Who knows, someone may invent a backyard nuclear fusion power plant by 2030 which will fit under your staircase or barbecue station, generating the worlds cheapest power which will render all existing power infrastructure obsolete.

If that happens, then transfer your investments to those firms which pioneer and more importantly establishes itself and leads in low cost decentralised power generation and distribution.

The existing power sector is more than 150 years old. I see its life limited to another 10 good years.

Decentralised power grids are the future. Centralised power grids like those of today are extremely vulnerable to Electromagnetic Pulse (EMP) attacks and will be the first to go down in the time of a war.

Other evergreen sectors are puncture proof tyres, agricultural commodities, agricultural food products for daily use, fast moving consumer goods (FMCG), steel, aluminium, healthcare, pharma, established innovative software behemoths that generate sales from innovation, services and product sales, and not mainly from advertising, and definitely not from the low cost outsourcing IT coolie model.

Other evergreen sectors are industries involved in the water sector(infrastructure, treatment, pollution control and distribution), telecommunications, video communications and any firm that comes up with teleportation like the original Star Trek series.

Star Trek was one of the most visionary TV series I have ever seen.

As a child, I loved Mr Spock of Star Trek more than I loved Batman, Lord Ram and Bhishma.

Star Trek showed cell phones and video communications in the 1960s itself. I think their vision of teleportation will also come true in the next 30 years (by 2050).

If you asked anybody in the 1960s, they would say cell phones and video conferencing is science fiction only possible in *Star Trek*.

But it came true in 2020.

If you ask anybody in the 2020s, they will say teleportation is science fiction only possible in *Star Trek*.

I chose to trust *Star Trek* based on their past track record.

Dealing with Armageddon 2026 and beyond

Note:

This article was originally written in 2017 and came true during Covid 2020.

I have slightly modified it to include 2024 conditions as I have revised some sections of the book in October 2024. The conditions I have mentioned below should occur by 2026 or 2028.

I may be off in the timing, but there is no doubt it will happen and cause a global reset and perhaps a way to go back to the future and #restorerealramrajya like I mentioned in my book **Arya Dharma** (https://aryadharma.world/).

People will be looking for a new way and I hope by God's grace my book Arya Dharma: The Noble Dharma will become viral (#restorerealramrajya #aryadharma) and show a better way by a unique combination of our heritage, spirituality and current affairs by going back to the future and restoring the glory of Bharat (India) and this world by returning to its ideals of Dharma and Seva.

My article before Covid 2020 below

The Everything Bubble has burst in 2020, just like the bubble of 2008, and preceded by the dotcom bubble of 2000.

Read my earlier article written on April 14, 2020 on the way forward after the China Virus Pandemic in 2020 (https://bit.ly/38jIVtL).

Below is a follow up to that article.

Real estate projects will be abandoned or sold like Lehman Brothers at hugely distressed rates.

Lehman Brothers was a fundamentally sound firm with a great history of over 150 years, which went bankrupt due to manipulations of senior government officials in collusion with the Wall Street Pimps and also because it was run purely by professionals and not by owners.

In the initial days of its bankruptcy, creditors of Lehman Brothers were only expected to receive 14 cents on the dollar.

That means for every dollar that they had invested; they would be paid back only 14 cents.

It is a different matter that Lehman Brothers was a 150 year old firm with immensely valuable assets and that it returned more than 38 cents on the dollar to its creditors.

The real estate market in Bharat has been a real estate speculators most orgasmic wet dream from the 1990s upto 2020. It has only seen an upside.

Bharat is the most overvalued real estate market in the world.

Bharat has not seen the bubble burst completely as of yet.

What has happened until June 2020, is not even a side show.

A highly paid person like my father earning 18 Sovereigns of gold per month could not afford it at 175 Sovereigns of gold even in 1980.

Which person earns 1071 Sovereigns of gold a year today in Bharat?

Only crooked politicians, bureaucrats and Wall Street/Dalal Street Pimps.

Their day of reckoning has come. All the real estate projects and real estate firms they invested their black money in will go bankrupt.

Real estate projects will be abandoned or sold like Lehman Brothers at hugely distressed rates.

Unlike Lehman Brothers, creditors in Bharat will not even receive 2 cents on the dollar.

That means for every dollar they invested; they will only be paid back 2 cents.

2 cents only if they are lucky, most likely all they will get is a rotten egg.

World over banks will collapse by 2022.

Below is a serious article on what is going to happen in the USA. It is already starting to happen.

The Looming Bank Collapse (https://bit.ly/2Ztjy4L)

More than 100 million loans in the USA have missed payments (https://bit.ly/2BuTf68)

The same thing will happen in Bharat and government banks will be the worst affected and the Bharatiya government will not be able to bail them out.

Bharat is a much weaker economy than the USA and you can imagine what is happening in Bharat right now. Banks even in Bharat will go bust as businesses and consumers fail to return loans.

The media in Bharat is paid and the NRI Business Development Manager is concealing all the bad news as his usual style.

Based on my Lehman Brothers experience, when a bank collapses all arms associated with the bank are hit including brokerage and mutual fund subsidiaries of the bank.

This will hit millions of investors especially the most poor and helpless who thought a fixed deposit in a government bank was the safest investment.

There will be riots on the streets.

Before this happens, by the end of 2020 or even sooner, or latest by 2021, the Representative DFIs and Wall Street/Dalal Street Pimps/Lalas will start World War 3, to distract people from what is really going on, and there is nothing like a World War to blame for all the bad that is happening and to inculcate a sense of patriotism and unity among the sheeple.

Finally, there will be bloody revolutions ignited in 2023, by a finally forcefully awakened sheeple which slept through the whole thing that was happening for the last 50 years, until they got kicked in the face themselves due to the manipulations of the Wall Street/Dalal Street Pimps/Lalas and the corrupt Representative DFIs and their flunkies and corrupt Sarkari Babus.

Instead of investing in material assets, people will be looking to invest in other people.

Investing in people is the most valuable investment a person can make.

To invest in people you do not need huge amounts of money.

In fact to invest in people, you do not need any money at all.

To invest in people you need the consistent practice of True Love, Dharma, SEVA (Selfless Sacrifice) and the things I have figured out.

The first people to invest in are your true family and true friends.

Your true family and true friends are not attracted to your wealth, they are attracted to you. They will be the only ones standing by you when you no longer have your wealth.

Your true family is not just your blood family, they are just products of your Karma.

From my personal experience, your blood family usually shows you fish love. Your true family and true friends give you true love, not fish love.

People will be looking for a new way and I hope by God's grace my book Arya Dharma: The Noble Dharma will become viral and show a better way by a unique combination of our heritage, spirituality and current affairs by going back to the future and restoring the glory of Bharat (India) and this world by returning to its ideals of Dharma and SEVA (selfless sacrifice).

By the time my son turns 18, we will return to the glory of Magadha in Bharat, and by the time his son turns 18 we will have Ram Rajya all over the world.

My son is going to be three in September 2020.

I am doing all this, not only for my son, but mainly for the children below 10 as of 2020.

They will be the greatest and most blessed generation this world has ever seen.

And if we sincerely follow what I have written in my book Arya Dharma: The Noble Dharma as soon as possible, our children will call us the greatest generation this world has ever seen.

Because we taught our children how to earn Real Wealth, which remains forever, not just material wealth which is ephemeral and will be lost to the sands of time.

By following my book Arya Dharma: The Noble Dharma we teach our children what Real Wealth is, and gave them the gift of immortality. *To never die.*

As the saying goes:

If you live in the hearts of those who we love, is to never die.

True Love and Real Wealth

What exactly is Fish Love?

The fish wants to swim and breathe and live in the waters.
It wants to be free to swim with other fish and chase its dreams.

You also love fish.
But you like to take it out of the water, kill it and fry and eat it.

You don't love the fish; you only love yourself.

If you truly loved the fish, you would get into the waters and swim with it.

You would let it live. You would follow it as it chased its dreams.

If you truly loved the fish, you would not take it out of the water, kill it and fry and eat it.

Check out the video below by Rabbi Dr. Abraham Twerski.

It will change your life.

Video of Rabbi Dr. Abraham Twerski On Love (https://youtu.be/CMcHtSjtNBY)

Refer to my article on what "Real Wealth" is.

The goal of "Real Wealth" is to become immortal. It is to never die. This is the ultimate goal of the Sanathan Dharma. This is the "Real Wealth".

To be remembered and loved for millenniums like Lord Ram, Jesus and the Sakyamuni.

As the saying goes:

If you live in the hearts of those who we love, is to never die.

This wealth does not come from just earning huge amounts of money.

This wealth can only be developed by the consistent practice of True Love, Dharma, SEVA (Selfless Service) and the things I have figured out.

Extracts from my book Arya Dharma: The Noble Dharma

Summary and Heart of my Work

Freedom is the ultimate power, and it is my divine birth right given to me by Brahman (God) to have freedom,
Freedom is not free,
Freedom comes from the blood, sweat and sacrifice of all worlds and all beings in all worlds,
Because the whole world is One Family.

And most importantly Freedom comes from the God given Karma (destiny) to be responsible and follow Dharma and its highest ideal SEVA (selfless service),
Because the Rtam (the Divine order) is the highest and only law of Brahman (God),
And the Rtam consists of doing our Karma to follow Dharma in our every breath,

Because Dharma defends those who defend it,
Dharma destroys those who destroy it,
Dharma can neither be created nor be destroyed.
You will reap what you sow.

If you understand hurting another being is adharma (violation of Dharma), loving and caring unselfishly without ego and expectations for another being is Dharma, you have performed Dharma.
Wherever there is a sacred people who adhere to Dharma, the land that they belong to automatically becomes blessed and it becomes Ram Rajya.

The root of happiness and well-being is Dharma.
The root of Dharma is Artha (economy and statecraft)

The root of Artha is good governance.
The root of good governance is conquering by self-control.
The root of conquering by self-control is humility.
The root of humility is SEVA (selfless service) to the old.
May there be well-being (auspiciousness) to the people;
May the kings always rule the earth with Dharma;
May the cows (& bulls) and the Arya (practitioner of Arya Dharma) always be fortunate.
May all the beings in all the worlds become happy;
May only peace remain in all worlds. (Om Shanthi, Shanti, Shanti)

O Absolute Truth and Creator of all three worlds,
May we contemplate on your unrivalled brilliance and divine light,
Guide our intellect so that we may be bestowed with True Knowledge.

O Absolute Truth and Creator of all three worlds, (Om)
Lead us from the unreal to the real,
Lead us from darkness unto light,
Lead us from death to Immortality,
May only peace remain in all worlds. (Om Shanthi, Shanti, Shanti)

Prologue/Introduction

Like most English educated children studying in Bharat in the 1980s and early 1990s, especially before the advent of the Internet, my view of Bharat was conditioned by Amar Chitra Katha comics, 80s Epics TV serials and our boring ICSE History textbooks.

It was only in my 20s, and especially after the advent of the internet and availability of online book buying in the mid-1990s, did I step outside the confines of this misguided influence and learn about our great history and heritage.

Bharata has the greatest history and heritage ever made by any civilisation in the history of the Universe.

It is a real shame to what we have become today because we blindly try to ape and emulate the fraud FUKUS (France, UK, USA) systems which are totally unsuitable not only to us, but to any country on this planet, including the FUKUS countries themselves, and especially harmful to this world and all beings in it and even more harmful to Nature, the supreme embodiment of Brahman.

It really makes you wonder about the state of this world when the priceless Amazon rain forest is valued at $20 million, and the Amazon online shopping website is valued at almost a trillion dollars.

There is something seriously long with such FUKUS systems that value money as the root of all happiness and place little or no value to Nature which is the greatest gift bestowed to use by Brahman, worth more than all the priceless treasures in all heavens.

There is something even more wrong with FUKUS systems that place money and power as the source of all law, and completely ignore and even trample, disregard, disrespect and wilfully violate the Rtam the divine law of Brahman of which Dharma and Karma are its fundamental components.

We had two golden eras after Ram Rajya:

- During the period of the Maurya's in the BCE Era

- During the period of Samudragupta and the Gupta Era in the CE Era.

If Bharat has to have any hope of restoring its past glory, it must abandon all the fraud FUKUS systems which place Self Interest as their guiding principle over Dharma and SEVA.

In FUKUS systems, self-interest rules and Dharma and SEVA (Selfless Service) is relegated only to their saints and prophets.

We must return to our eternal guiding principles that were laid down ever since Ram Rajya of Dharma and SEVA or Selfless Service which were the guiding principles of the Golden Era of Bharat, especially during the time of the Maurya's when we surpassed even the Roman and Greek empires and made Alexander retreat in fearful haste without even daring to fight us.

If Bharat must have any hope of restoring its past glory, it must abandon the fraud FUKUS systems which place only money and self-interest as their guiding principle, and return to Dharma and SEVA (Selfless Service) which were our eternal guiding principles that were laid down ever since Ram Rajya.

Dharma and SEVA were the guiding principles of the Golden Era of Bharat, when we surpassed even the Roman, Greek and Persian empires and even made a world conqueror like Alexander retreat in fearful haste without even daring to fight us.

If the systems mentioned in this publication are adopted in the world, it would surely lead to a Utopian Society where there is no king, religion, greed, and selfishness and all the subjects would be governing themselves following the highest order of Dharma called Arya Dharma (The Noble Dharma).

This book contains my life's learning not only from books, but more importantly from living in the USA and Bharat and dealing with its common citizens and governments on a daily basis.

I have seen the best and the worst of both the USA and Bharat, but choose to live and die in Bharat, because we still have a sense of morals and values and don't worship money as the ultimate satisfaction, despite all our so-called flaws.

I doubt if rude, crude, characterless men and serial rapists like Trump or even Bill Clinton would ever be elected as supreme leaders of Bharat.

Instead despite all the flaws of our politicians, we still manage to elect men like S Radhakrishnan and APJ Abdul Kalam as our supreme leaders and still respect, honour and cherish Anna Hazare and Swami Vivekananda and hold them in higher regard than Mukesh Ambani or Vijay Mallaya.

I hope this book will lead people to my website www.aryadharma.world which is a far more interactive experience than reading this book. The twitter tag for this book is #restorerealramrajya

Nothing I have predicted is my great genius alone.

It is also apparent for millenniums, to millions of people like me who do not place self-interest and making money as their prime goal in life.

These millions of people realise that unconditional love and devotion of all of Brahman's creation, non-attachment to this material world, Dharma and SEVA (Selfless Service) to all beings in this world are alone the keys to Happiness.

MK Gandhi saw this, Swami Vivekananda and Tagore saw this in the early 1900s, and our ancestors saw this more than 10000 years ago when we had real Ram Rajya because they practiced the above under the living example of Lord Ram who sacrificed his own wife and unborn children for the sake of Dharma.

Once a disciple walked up to the Sakyamuni (Gauthama Buddha) and said:
I want Happiness.

The Sakyamuni said:
Drop the "I" and the "Want" and all you are left with is "Happiness".

The "I" is Ego. The "Want" is selfish desire, instead of selfless action of SEVA (Selfless Sacrifice). The main key to Happiness is to do everything without expectations and without ego.

Apply this golden rule to every facet of your life and you will immediately drop the heavy baggage of expectations and all the associated disappointment that comes with it when your expectations are not met or when your ego is hurt.

Thanks again for your support.

I hope you understand the true goal of my work, and it changes your life and you find Real Wealth and Real Happiness and tell others also how to find it.

How to Identify a True Leader

A true leader should be like Lord Ram.

Lord Ram was not just a God, but an ideal for all of humanity for not just millenniums, but for posterity.

I suggest the first book on leadership that should be **taught in all schools**, not just management schools, is the Yoga Vasistha which formed the character of Rama and then the Shri Ramcharitamanas by Tulasidas which is the life story of what Rama actually did after his character was formed.

I have the version that is translated and edited by RC Prasad and I recommend it since it has the original Avadhi text, Hindi translation and English translation.

There is also a very good website of the Shri Ramacharitamanas (http://www.ramcharitmanas.org/) that I found recently.

You can also download a PDF of the book from https://holybooks.com/sri-ram-charita-manas-the-ramayana-of-goswami-tulasidas-pdf/

Nobody can be completely like Lord Ram.

A divine being like Lord Ram is born only once as an ideal for humanity.

But if a person has even 60% of the main characteristics I have mentioned below, they will be good leaders. A combination of many such leaders can restore Ram Rajya in the entire world.

Even if we cannot achieve Ram Rajya, let us identify leaders who can at least help us achieve what Thomas Paine said:

When shall it be said in any country of the world,
My poor are happy, neither ignorance or distress is to be found among them;
My jails are empty of prisoners, my streets of beggars;
The aged are not in want,
The taxes not oppressive;
The rational world is my friend because I am friend of its happiness.
When these things can be said, then may that country boast of its constitution and government.

My main identification characteristics to identify True Leaders comes from reading our traditional scriptures of the Sanathan Dharma in Bharat, especially the Yoga Vasistha, Shri Ramcharitamanas, the Mahabharat especially the Shanthi Parva and the Bhagavad Gita and the folk tales of Rama like the tale of Rama and the Squirrel and the tale of Rama and the Dog among the many other tales I have heard of Rama.

 1. A true leader will walk the talk.

Word and action should be one like Paravathi and Parameshwara(Shiva).

Above is a very famous saying from Kalidasa who was the greatest poet and playwright ever in the history of the world.

For a person to be truly united in word and action, they should have achieved समत्वम् (Samathvam) and this only comes from sincere and sustained practice of ध्यान Dhyan.

A true leader will be the first to walk the talk. If they declare war on another country, they will be the first to fight in the trenches along with the rest of their troops. They will get their hands dirty. They will not believe in remote control leadership. If they want something done, they will do it themselves first as an example.

People say Rama fought Ravana. Not for land, not for money, not for oil, not for gold, not for ego but to rescue his own wife who was kidnapped by Ravana.

That is why there was Ram Rajya.

2. Adherence to Dharma and its highest ideal of SEVA (Selfless Service) will matter more to a leader than money or adherence to GDP.

What exactly is Dharma?

The concept of Dharma is best explained in the various books of the Sanathan Dharma .

There is no correct English translation of the word Dharma. The closest meaning is a virtuous way of conduct and living but this is not even a 20% completely accurate nor comprehensive translation.

The Uttharkanda section of the Ram Charitra Manas has described Dharma in the most succinct manner that can be understood by all.

According to Lord Ram:
Brother, there is no greater Dharma than benevolence (परहित), no greater sin than oppressing others.
I have declared to you, dear brother, the verdict of all the Vedas and the Puranas, and the learned also know it.

Benevolence means altruism or selflessness and being always concerned about and working for the welfare of others.

परहति is a very complicated word.

A simpler meaning is निस्वारथ सेवा or simply सेवा (SEVA). सेवा (SEVA) means Selfless Service.

So the highest Dharma is सेवा (SEVA) or Selfless Service not just to humanity, but to the whole world.

Because the highest ideal of the Sanathan Dharma is:

वसुधैव कुटुम्बकम् *(Vasudhaiva Kutumbakam)*

The whole world is One Family.

There is another important definition of Dharma according to one of the greatest philosophers of modern times.

What is Dharma?

```
If you understand hurting another man is
adharma (violation of Dharma), pleasing
another man is Dharma, you have performed
Dharma.
S Radhakrishnan, 2nd President of India.
```

3. A true leader will value small grains of sand and minute powder particles of cement the same as mighty rock because you need all of them to make concrete. I got this lesson from the story of Rama and the Squirrel and how the squirrel got its three stripes. It is a

very interesting story. Read it here. This is a folk tale of Rama and not found either in Valmiki's Ramayana or in Tulasi Das's Shri Ramcharitamanas.

Rama's lesson from the story:

Rama continued, "Always remember, however small, every task is equally important. Great work can never be completed by a few people alone. It needs the support of all, and however small, an effort should always be appreciated.

Rama lovingly held the squirrel close to him. He turned to the monkeys and gravely said, "Do not make fun of the weak and the small. Your strength or what you do is not important. What matters is your love. This little squirrel has love in its heart."

"O monkeys, you are brave and strong and doing a wonderful job bringing all these huge boulders and stones from far away and dropping them in the ocean. But did you notice the tiny pebbles and stones that this small squirrel and other smaller creatures have brought are filling the small gaps between the huge stones? Do you not realise that the tiny grains of sand brought by this squirrel are the ones that bind the whole structure and make it strong? Yet you scold this small creature and fling it away in anger!"

Hearing this, the monkeys were ashamed
and bowed their heads in embarrassment.

4. A true leader will be spiritual, not moral.
Morality is like a laser light, powerful, focused and intense, which eventually blinds and disables you, and it mainly has darkness all outside its narrow and specialised area of focus.

While spirituality is like the light of a candle, soft, warm and spreading light all around it, even to the darkest of corners and you enjoy the warmth and glow of the candle.

5. A true leader can be consistently trusted and consistently earns that trust only by their consistent and sincere actions, and not just by their words.

6. A true leader does not object to, and readily accepts verification of trust bestowed upon them.

7. A true leader will be mainly inspired by sincere and humane ideals, and not mainly by monetary rewards or considerations.

8. A true leader will not consider themselves indispensable nor will they regard others as indispensable, but they will recognise, honour, treasure and value loyalty, devotion, and sacrifice.

9. A true leader will listen to learn. They accept criticism, have an open mind and can even pivot 180 degrees from their original position if they see value in another's opinion even if it is contrary to their own previously held opinion.

10. A true leader will only make promises they can keep otherwise they will just say no.

11. A true leader will not fight with violence (forcefully) unless they have exhausted all other options and absolutely have no other option.

According to the Sanathan Dharma there are four stages of fighting:

- Sama (try to befriend or form alliance)
- Dana (give gifts, presents and do favours)
- Bheda (confuse, deceive, separate, divide and rule)
- And finally, when all else fails Dhand (military or physical force).

12. A true leader won't decide punishment, they will leave the punishment to the victim to decide. I learnt this story from the tale of Rama and the Dog. Rama gave an audience and hearing for justice even to a dog who was a victim of a merciless beating by an offender. Rama let the dog decide the punishment to be given to the offender. According to Rama, the victim best knows what punishment to mete out to an offender. This is assuming the victim is doing this out of their free and informed and unforced consent and given a cooling off period of at least 3 months for serious offences before meting out the punishment.

13. A true leader will never consider themselves as superior to others, they will wear their humility and ordinariness lightly and always on their sleeve.

14. A true leader will have समत्वम् (Samathvam or Equanimity). They will have empathy and treat all beings equally with love and kindness. I say all beings, not just human beings. Lord Ram gave justice and utmost respect even to a dog.

15. A true leader will not exempt themselves or their family or loved ones from punishment if they have violated Dharma or the laws of the land.

16. A true leader will realise that if you don't first successfully invest in people, you will never be able to invest in anything successfully.

Investing in people is the most valuable investment a person can make.

To invest in people, you do not need huge amounts of money.

In fact, to invest in people, you do not need any money at all.
To invest in people you need the consistent practice of True Love, Dharma, SEVA (Selfless Service) and the things I have figured out.

17. A true leader will place the highest goal of the Arthasastra– SEVA to the old as the highest ideal of Dharma.

सुखस्य मूलं धर्मः ।

धर्मस्य मूलं अर्थः ।

अर्थस्य मूलं राज्यं ।

राज्यस्य मूलं इन्द्रयि जयः ।

इन्द्रयियाजयस्य मूलं वनियः ।

वनियस्य मूलं वृद्धोपसेवा॥

The root of happiness and well being is Dharma.
The root of Dharma is Artha (economy and statecraft)

```
The root of Artha is good governance.
The root of good governance is conquering by
self control.
The root of conquering by self control is
humility.
The root of humility is SEVA (selfless
service) to the old.
```

18. A true leader will recognise sacrifice and they will:
    - Be aware of who sacrificed what and how much.
    - Remain grateful for life towards those who sacrificed their well being for the well being of others.
    - Make serious attempts to offer compensation, support and a permanent replacement of income to those sacrificed themselves, for at least 3 generations of their families.

19. A true leader will try to convince, not command into obedience.
    After all the Gita was explained, Lord Krishna said:

    ```
    I have given you my wisdom, it is for you
    to do as you think fit.
    ```

20. Never make a money counter a leader, a money counter is just a monkey and monkeys are only to perform tricks and to be paid only in peanuts.
    Great things came not from counting money, but from passionate hearts and devotion to sincere ideals.

21. Never make a smooth talker or "Brilliant Orator" a leader, a smooth talker usually does not walk their talk.

22. **A true leader will focus on earning respect, not attention.**

23. **A true leader will focus on earning loyalty, not obedience.**

24. **A true leader will realise that age and authority does not mean automatic respect.**

Below is one of the best motivational videos I have watched on life and leadership. You can watch all of Simon Sineks videos at https://www.youtube.com/user/SimonSinek
https://www.youtube.com/watch?v=4DA82guEXSQ

I wish I read this excellent article by NK Carlson on the qualities of a bad leader. It is an eye opener and warning never to work for a bad leader.

Extracts from the article:
Transparency
Good leaders communicate transparently, but only to the point of necessity. Bad leaders communicate either too transparently or not transparently enough.

Compassionate
Good leaders communicate with compassion. Bad leaders communicate with no compassion. When bad leaders communicate, they do not take the feelings of others into consideration. Bad leaders communicate in a way that is cold and distant. The root of this is those bad leaders don't actually care about anyone other than themselves and their own power.

Along with this, bad leaders will never say, "I'm sorry." They won't say they are sorry for something they did, they won't even say they are sorry that a situation is bad. A bad leader never apologizes.

On the other hand, a good leader cares about people and takes others' feelings into account. Most importantly, a good leader communicates bad news in a way where employees leave the conversation knowing the leader cares about them.

Answers   *Questions*

A good leader is helpful and answers questions and concerns. A bad leader ignores questions or dances around them. This goes with the transparency issue above. A bad leader will withhold information for their own purposes. Even when you could be transparent and give answers, they will not, especially when those answers would undermine their power. A bad leader is far from helpful. In many cases, a bad leader will ignore questions or even attack question askers.

A good leader welcomes questions and answers each one, even if that answer is, "I'm sorry, I am unable to answer that question due to confidentiality." A good leader wants more information available rather than less. A good leader wants to foster understanding when decisions are made. A good leader will help their employees understand through questions and answers. A good leader has nothing to hide about how a decision is made and why.

Clarity

Above all, good leaders seek to communicate with clarity. Bad leaders do not seek clarity, because many times, a bad leader makes decisions that would not pass scrutiny. Ironically, bad leaders may use more words to communicate decisions.

A good leader will communicate clearly in as few words as possible because they know that many words often bring more fog than clarity. A good leader is direct. Listening is also a sign of good communication. A good communicator listens to concerns rather than monopolizing the conversation so they can better address those concerns. Good communicators and leaders know that face-to-face conversation is usually the best way to communicate, especially when communicating bad news.

Good leaders choose the proper medium so that clarity can be maximized.

ध्यान Dhyana

According to the Gita and the Brahmasutra, ब्रह्मन् (Brahman) can only be reached by those who practice and follow ध्यान (Dhyan or Dhyana).

Even Saint Pio of Peitrelcina said:

Through the study of books, one seeks God,

By meditation (ध्यान (Dhyana)), one finds him.

Dhyana or (Raja) Yoga is the highest of all yogas – to become a person balanced in all actions and thoughts.

One who has achieved समत्वमं Samathvam (Equanimity or Balance).

The perfect description of the ध्यान yoga is given in the Gita.

This is what the Gita says about one who has mastered the ध्यान Yoga:

The Yogin is greater than the Ascetic, he is considered greater than the man of knowledge, greater than the man of ritual works.

Bhagavad Gita 6.46

Sankara Acharya says that ध्यान can only be done by a person who has renounced everything in the world and is not possible to be achieved by a Grihastha (householder).

A person who sincerely and consistently practices ध्यान will realise the true form of ब्रह्मन् which is mainly समत्वम् Samathvam (equanimity), compassion and mercy.

You will only bring out your divine nature and develop Samathvam (equanimity), compassion and mercy to achieve oneness with ब्रह्मन् (Brahman) by the sincere and sustained practice of ध्यान (Dhyan or Dhyana).

It does not matter which religion you belong to; all religions finally preach the same thing:

Oneness or Union with Brahman and Brahman's creation.

Once you achieve follow and practice ध्यान (Dhyana) and achieve Oneness with Brahman, you achieve the highest goal and ideal in the Gita: *समत्वम् Samathvam or Equanimity.*

The Bhagavad Gita says in (II.48):

"Perform your duty with equanimity, O Arjuna, abandoning all attachment to success or failure.

Such equanimity (Samathvam) is called Yoga."

समत्वम् योग उच्यते (Samathvam Yoga Ucyate)

But what is action?

The Gita says:

He who sees inaction in action and action in inaction is wise among men.

Action means doing your duty without attachment to the fruits of your actions and always dedicated to Brahman.

You must do your duty regardless of what will happen to the results and without any expectation of the fruits of that action.

The Viṣṇu Puraṇa says:

That is action, which does not promote attachment; that is knowledge which liberates.

All other action is a mere effort/hardship; all other knowledge is merely another skill/craftsmanship.

What is duty?

Duty is the complete surrender to Brahman(God) and performance of all your actions with Samathvam (equanimity) to uphold the Dharma.

What is ध्यान?

No Thing – Attachment to no thing.

As the Gita says:

The enlightened, Brahman abiding,

Calm-hearted, unbewildered,

Is neither elated by the pleasant

Nor saddened by the unpleasant

What does attachment to No Thing mean?

Attachment to No Thing, means that you must give unconditionally without any expectations.

We are all human and will feel elated or depressed and this is acceptable, but we should not get lost for a long time in this elation or depression.

We must live in the moment, and the moment is only in the present.

No attachment or detachment means that one must be involved but not entangled.

As Imam Ali said:

Detachment is not that you should own nothing, but nothing should own you

ध्यान can be used both for good and for bad.

When you are detached you can either become a selfless saint, or sometimes a solider willing to kill a noble stranger for the sake of his nation, or even worse a psychopathic murderer willing to kill for his pleasure.

Hence first develop clarity of purpose. Then practice ध्यान with clarity of purpose.

What is clarity of purpose?

Clarity of purpose is to always follow the Dharma.

What is Dharma?

If you understand hurting another man is adharma (violation of Dharma), pleasing another man is Dharma, you have performed Dharma.

S Radhakrishnan, 2nd President of Bharat.

I firmly believe that most criminals and Wicked can reform if they realise the folly of their actions and this realisation comes with the sincere and sustained practice of ध्यान (Dhyana).

I firmly believe that the thorough, sincere and sustained practice of ध्यान must be introduced in all prisons and all prisoners must be encouraged it to practice it daily or if possible, twice daily before sunrise and after sunset.

I firmly believe all people especially the Brahma Dana and those who are depressed and have other mental illnesses must also be introduced to the thorough, sincere and sustained practice of

ध्यान and encouraged it to practice it daily or if possible twice daily before sunrise and after sunset.

I am a personal living testament to the power of ध्यान to recover from the fraud gutter pseudo "science" of Psychiatry.

For those of you who think what I say is all hocus pocus, wishy washy philosophical mumbo jumbo, for scientific validation listen to the below video by Dr Richard Davidson, a pioneering neuroscientist who has scientific proof that ध्यान (loosely translated as meditation) improves mental wellbeing right at the genetic level and induces happiness, kindness and compassion.

Video of Wellbeing is a Skill: Richard Davidson (https://youtu.be/EPGJU7W0N0I)

Once people are introduced to ध्यान they will no longer need intoxicants like drinking and smoking and drugs.

Sincere and sustained practice of ध्यान gives a person a permanent sense of wellbeing with wonderful side effects of being concerned for the wellbeing of others and all creation in this world.

This is unlike other intoxicants which only have temporary highs and harmful side effects and bring ruin and misery not only to oneself but also to one's family.

In chapter 6 of the Bhagavad Gita, ध्यान is a must to realize God.

In the Buddhist texts ध्यान (Zen) is a must to obtain Nirvana.

The supreme Ideal of the Sat Yuga, the Arya era of the golden age of truth is ध्यान (Dhyana).

ध्यान does not mean stop thinking or close your eyes or breathe slowly to relax.

Before one begins to do ध्यान, one must be calm and relaxed.

People have it all backwards, you don't practice ध्यान to relax, you relax to practice ध्यान.

True ध्यान is very difficult to achieve.

But ध्यान (Dhyan) is the only path to Nirvana and Moksha which leads to the realisation and final unity of the Atma with ब्रह्मन् (Brahman).

Close not your eye and thoughts, but close your senses to attachment and Vasanas.

Truly mastering ध्यान means achieving समत्वमं Samathvam or equanimity.

समत्वमं Samathvam and ध्यान Dhyan are interchangeable. One cannot exist without the other.

But समत्वमं Samathvam can only come from practice of ध्यान Dhyan.

Once you reach समत्वम् Samathvam, you unite with Brahman and achieve Moksha (NO THING or (Shunyata). Moksha means freedom from Vasanas and from the permanent influence of Karma.

So it is all about nothing. After all the hard work you put in to understand and practice ध्यान hopefully you would have achieved nothing.

समत्वम् Samathvam

What exactly is समत्वम् Samathvam?

समत्वम् Samathvam is Yoga.

Once you achieve समत्वम् Samathvam (Equanimity) you become a Yogin (Yogi).

Becoming a Yogin is the highest ideal of the Gita and the highest ideal of mankind and humanity.

This is what the Gita says about one who has mastered the ध्यान Yoga and achieved समत्वम् Samathvam:

The Yogin is greater than the Ascetic,

he is considered greater than the man of knowledge,

greater than the man of ritual works.

Bhagavad Gita 6.46

As Shyam Sundar Goswami said in his wonderful book about his named Master's teaching:

A yogi can be in the forests of the Himalaya or in a big city;

*a   real yogi is   unconcerned   with   his   own
environment as he is with himself.*

A person who sincerely and consistently practices ध्यान will realise the true form of ब्रह्मन् which is mainly समत्वम् Samathvam, compassion and mercy.

You will only bring out your divine nature and develop समत्वम् Samathvam, compassion and mercy to achieve oneness with ब्रह्मन् (Brahman) by the sincere and sustained practice of ध्यान (Dhyan or Dhyana).

It does not matter which religion you belong to; all religions finally preach the same thing:

*Oneness   or   Union   with Brahman and   Brahman's
creation.*

Once you achieve follow and practice ध्यान (Dhyan) and achieve Oneness with Brahman, you achieve the highest goal and ideal in the Gita:

समत्वम् Samathvam or Equanimity.

Real Wealth

What is Real Wealth?

Does it just mean billions in paper money?

Does it mean just thousands of acres of land and tonnes of gold?

Even a world conqueror like Alexander, who spent his whole life travelling thousands of kilometres and destroying millions of lives in the pursuit of land, gold and wealth, finally realised the truth:

The second wish of strewing gold, silver, and other riches on the way to the graveyard is to tell people that not even a fraction of gold will come with me.

I spent all my life earning riches but cannot take anything with me.

Let people realize that it is a sheer waste of time to chase wealth.

And about my third wish of having my hands dangling out of the coffin, I wish people to know that I came empty handed into this world and empty handed I go out of this world.

This is what the Bhaja Govindam says about so called "wealth":

arthamanartham bhaavaya nityam
naastitatah sukhaleshah satyam
putraadapi dhana bhaajaam bhiitih
sarvatraishhaa vihiaa riitih

*Wealth is not welfare, truly there is no joy
in it.*
Reflect thus at all times.
A rich man fears even his own son.
This is the way of wealth everywhere.
Video of Bhaja Govindam -- Sanskrit Hymn with English Meanings
-- M.S.Subbulakshmi :https://youtu.be/z7RR73532OQ

Ben Zoma said:

Who is rich? He who is satisfied with his lot.

Epictetus said:

*Wealth   consists   not   in   having   great
possessions, but in having few wants.*

Does anybody even know how much money Jesus, Lord Ram and
the Sakyamuni had?

Forget about remembering their wealth, does anybody even
remember who the richest men were in the times of Jesus, Lord
Ram and the Sakyamuni?

What was it that Jesus, Lord Ram, and the Sakyamuni had that
makes them remembered, loved, emulated, honoured and respected
even to this day?

It was the strength of their character, accomplishments, happiness
they brought to others and their consistent practice of Dharma,
selflessness and compassion to others even at the cost of their own
selves.

*The true wealth of a person lies in the
betterment and happiness they brought to whose*

lives they touched and in the memories of those who they love.

As the saying goes:

If you live in the hearts of those who we love, is to never die.

This wealth does not come from just earning huge amounts of money.

This wealth can only be developed by the consistent practice of True Love, Dharma, SEVA (Selfless Sacrifice) and the things I have figured out.

The goal of "Real Wealth" is to become immortal. It is to never die.

This is the ultimate goal of the Sanathan Dharma. This is the "Real Wealth". To never die.

Things I have Figured Out

- *Golden saying of Sarvajna:*
  ```
  Learn some from those who know,
  Learn some from those who do,
  and rest you learn from Self Experience.
  ```

- *Learn who Brahman (God) truly is.*

Remember man made "religion", not God (Brahman).

Brahman did not create for "religion", colour, caste, or creed.

Brahman created not just for all humanity, but for this whole world which includes all living beings and the magnificent and splendid wonder and glory of nature.

- *Love and respect and Brahman's creation as much as you love Brahman.*

- *Always have faith in Brahman, faith in yourself and faith in the goodwill of your fellowman.*

- *The only thing that is constant, final and absolute is the Rtam.*

The Rtam is the most absolute, perfect and divine law of Brahman.

Dharma along with Karma are the important and fundamental components of the Rtam.

- *Practice ध्यान (Dhyan) for at least 30 minutes in a day.*

Do this not to relax for a few minutes, but to achieve समत्वम् (Samathvam) in your entire daily life.

What is समत्वम् (Samathvam)?

समत्वम् (Samathvam) is Yoga.

Once you achieve समत्वम् (Samathvam) you become a Yogi.

As Shyam Sundar Goswami said in his wonderful book about his unnamed Master's teaching:

A yogi can be in the forests of the Himalaya or in a big city;

a real yogi is unconcerned with his own environment as he is with himself.

- *Find at least 30 minutes a day for Hatha Yoga, or at least 15 rounds of Suryanamaskar or at least a 20 minute run.*
- *Practice the main key to Happiness. Learn to have no expectations in every action you do.*
- *Selfishness and Ego are the root cause of all suffering and evil in this world.*

Never have an ego and never be selfish and inconsiderate. Help the weakest of people and treat them as your equal with love and respect.

In the eyes of Brahman, all are equal.

It is the Rtam that makes people unequal. The Rtam is a continuous wheel.

The wheel of Justice.

If you are not selfish, inconsiderate and do not have an ego, you will have the world at your feet and the whole world will love you and respect you and some may even die for you.

Ironically, having people die for them was actually main intention of a selfish and egotistical person in the first place.

- *Investing in people is the most valuable investment a person can make.*
  To invest in people, you don't need huge amounts of money.

  In fact, to invest in people, you don't need any money at all.

  To invest in people you need the consistent practice of True Love, Dharma, SEVA (Selfless Sacrifice) and the things I have figured out.

  The first people to invest in are your true family and true friends.

  Your true family and true friends are not attracted to your wealth, they are attracted to you. They will be the only ones standing by you when you no longer have your wealth.

  Your true family is not just your blood family, they are just products of your Karma.

  From my personal experience, your blood family usually shows you fish love.

  Your true family and true friends give you true love, not fish love.

- *Only ignorant idiots take pride in the feeling of "I" and "my" and "only mine".*

It is only a world class ignorant dumbass who thinks the world begins and ends with only "I", "my" and "only mine".

It is an even more world class ignorant Six Sigma quality dumbass who thinks that they are immortal and can continue what they are doing forever.

It is an even more world class ignorant Kaizen Six Sigma quality dumbass who thinks that they can continue to dictate what the world should do even after they are gone.

Nothing you consider "yours" is really yours.

Your name was given to you by your mother.

Whether you like it or not, one day all your family would have left you.

That includes your mother and father who will eventually pass way, your siblings who will have their own families to look after, and your children who will wander off to chase their own dreams.

All that will be left is you and your spouse.

And one day, even your spouse will grow old and die.

And finally on the ultimate day, whether you like it or not you will be forced to leave your body.

Even if you are sorry for being forced to leave on that ultimate day, be extremely thankful if you first did not already end up blind, toothless, wearing adult diapers and probably not remembering when you ate your last meal, and not even remembering the name of your favourite child.

All the so called "wealth" you earned and proudly claimed as only yours, will one day be lost by your heirs who took their inheritance for granted.

Even worse, the so called "wealth" that you earned, may be thrown back in your face by your heirs, and abandoned to the wilderness if you aim to force your wishes on your heirs even after your gone.

And as I have said many times:

Anything that is taken for granted is usually lost, discarded, or abandoned.

The only thing that is truly yours are the memories you leave behind in the ones who you truly love.

That is your only real wealth.

- *Learn to treasure the value of things, not the price of them.*

Some of the most precious things in life are "free".

Love, compassion, trust, kindness, honesty, respect, faith, devotion, sincerity, sacrifice, goodwill, benevolence, the splendour and glory of Nature, and many other such intangible but priceless and invaluable things have no intrinsic "price".

There is no price on them, they are given freely and generously.

Would you really prefer to take all the money and gold in the world, and not bother to have even one of what I have mentioned above, because they have no price and are given freely and generously?

Never ever maintain any relationship with any person who only measures you by the money or wealth or assets you have.

Once your money and wealth are gone, that person will also be gone.

- *Never ever maintain any relationship with any person who only measures you by the money or wealth or assets you have.*

- *If the only problem is money, it is not a problem at all.*

Money comes and goes and comes again.

Anybody who loses heart because they do not have money, is making a big mistake.

I know some people who have even committed suicide because they had no money.

There are much worse things in life to lose than money – health, your sense of wellbeing, your very consciousness of self, your reputation, kindness, solidarity, and goodwill of others and most importantly the trust, love and respect of those you love.

As long as you have the above, money should be the least of your worries.

- *Money while necessary motivates neither the best people nor the best in people. Purpose does*

A wonderful quote by Vala Afshar.

- *Do not waste your time trying to offer a diamond to a pig.*

There is absolutely no use offering a diamond to a pig.

It would step right over it, crush it into the filthy mud, and still prefer to wallow in filthy mud and eat slop.

Love, compassion, trust, kindness, honesty, respect, faith, devotion, sacrifice, sincerity, goodwill, benevolence, the splendour and glory of Nature and many other such intangible but priceless and invaluable things have no intrinsic "price".

But the things I have mentioned above are more valuable than all the gold and diamonds, not just in the earth, but in the Multiverse.

They should only be offered to people who recognise its value.

- *You only realise the value of something or someone when you lose them.*
- *Learn to recognise what true love is before you give or take it.*

True love is to give without expectations.

Even more true love is to do for someone what they want to do, not what you want them to do.

- *Love means nothing without trust first, and then respect.*

Trust is the most important relationship.

Then comes Respect. Only if you have trust and respect for a person does your love really mean something.

Without trust and respect, thinking somebody loves you is just a pointless delusion.

It is a two-way pointless delusion:

You are deluded to think they really care about you and they are deluded to think they really care about you.

- *Be honest – Trust can only be earned if one is honest.*

Never lie, cheat or steal except for the protection of Dharma.

If you do not want to talk about anything, don't lie, just say "No Comment" like most diplomats do.

Or better yet, say:

"That's for me to know and you to find out".

Of course there are exceptions.

If somebody held a gun to your head and asked you for the address of your friend who he wanted to murder, then you can lie about your friend's address.

- *Trust is the supreme relationship.*

Trust is the fundamental basis of any relationship.

You cannot truly love or respect anybody unless you trust them first.

This applies even to your closest family including your parents, siblings, spouse, and children.

Unless you trust them first, all your other proclaimed "relationships" with them are worthless.

It is like trying to build a house on a foundation of sand.

Even a dog shed cannot be built on a foundation of sand.

Trust is that rock solid foundation over which you can build the world's tallest skyscrapers and worlds' strongest castles, dams, and forts.

- *Trust but Verify.*

It is better to trust but verify, than never trust at all.

If somebody trusts you, they have every right to verify that trust.

But in the same measure, never blindly trust anybody without verifying their underlying intentions and motives.

Especially in legal, financial and contractual matters where your own reputation is at stake, or even worse, you can become bankrupt, be held liable, or even be imprisoned, do not trust even your own father, brother, sister, son, daughter or even spouse without verifying their underlying intentions.

The most grievous and serious of losses and even death to a person was caused because of betrayal, not by their enemies, but by those they considered closest to them, their own family including fathers, brothers, sons, and spouses.

Usually the only person who will never betray you is your mother.

But sometimes even honest mothers lead the way to hell with their selfish, egotistical, and ignorant intentions.

Most of the marriages of those I know who failed, were mainly because of problems with the mother-in-law.

- *Word and action should be one like Paravathi and Parameshwara (Shiva).*

Above is a very famous saying from Kalidasa who was the greatest poet and playwright ever in the history of the world.

For a person to be truly united in word and action, they should have achieved समत्वम् (Samathvam) and this only comes from sincere and sustained practice of ध्यान Dhyan.

- *Watch what you speak and write.*

There is a saying in Kannada:

```
A pearl once broken cannot be taken back, and
words once spoken (or written) cannot be taken
back.
```

I personally know relationships that were built over years that were completely destroyed because of harsh words either verbally or written spoken in impulse and anger.

Verbal harshness is far more damaging especially if you do it in public and humiliate another person in front of a crowd.

Any person who cannot control impulsive harsh words and actions is not fit to be a leader or a manager of people and is only fit to be a low level technician or solitary worker who should not be allowed to interact with people or even animals and plants.

Such harsh, impulsive, selfish, self-centred, and disrespectful people are only fit to interact with machines or dig ditches or break stones.

People do not leave good companies; they leave bad managers.

- *The trouble with most of us is that we would rather be ruined by praise than saved by criticism.*

This is a very famous saying by Americas most famous motivational speaker Norman Vincent Peale.

- *Focus on earning loyalty, not obedience.*

Obedience comes from fear, loyalty comes from the heart.

Loyalty can only be earned by consistently practicing Dharma, and being just and fair and equal towards all without favouritism or nepotism.

Loyalty is not a one-way street — it is reciprocal, you must be the first one to stand and last one to leave to those who stand by you.

In fact if you were truly loyal, you would never leave at all.

However it must be known that in transactional affairs (where there is a monetary component involved) – e.g. employment or business relationships, many a times these affairs become transactional — when the person is no longer capable of compensating somebody, they will leave.

Hence loyalty in transactional affairs can only be given upto the point a person will be putting their own wellbeing at risk to remain loyal.

Whereas in affairs where there is no transactional component, loyalty can be placed upto whatever the other level of loyalty the other person is willing to commit.

As I mentioned before in my article on the Raja Rishi (Sage King):

Only a just king commands the loyalty of people.

The subjects of a just king attacked by another will follow him until death, even if he is weak.

On the other hand, when a strong but unjust king is attacked, his people will either topple him or go over to the enemy.

- *Focus on earning respect, not attention.*

Barking dogs get attention, sleeping lions get respect.

So if a person is to earn respect, they need to develop qualities that are worth respecting and this only comes from the practice of Dharma, and development of some ability of competence with devotion, intelligence, talent, hard and smart work.

- *Age and authority does not mean automatic respect.*

Respect has to be earned by developing good Gunas (Character) and Karma(conduct), not demanded automatically by position or age.

- *Learn to recognise and work for good leadership and never work for bad leadership.*

- *If you have nothing to hide, you have nothing to fear.*

Ironically this was said by Goebbels who built his whole life by creating fear and hiding the real truth of the Nazi's work.

- *Always be good and kind to people who have nothing to lose.*

When a person has nothing to lose, they can either become a great saint or a dangerous suicide bomber.

The most dangerous suicide bomber is one who feels he has nothing to lose so he gives away his life freely in the form of hate for all mankind.

The most wonderful saint is one who feels he has nothing to lose, so he gives away his life freely in the form of love for not just mankind but the whole world.

Love and hate are not inborn qualities.

They are developed by a person's interaction with the world around them.

If a person has only been shown hate, he will become a hateful person.

If a person has only been shown love, he will become a lovable person.

- *SEVA is only done selflessly.*

True SEVA is to be good and kind to people from you have nothing to gain, not even a thank you.

SEVA or selfless service is not returning a favour for somebody who has done you a favour.

SEVA is also not doing a favour for someone you care about or somebody who you think is important.

SEVA or selfless service is the most selfish form of service.

As the Dalai Lama said:

My advice is that if you must be selfish, be wisely selfish.

Wise people serve others sincerely, putting the needs of others above their own. Ultimately you will be happier.

If you want to be truly selfish, help someone.

- *People perform their best and give their heart and soul when given the promise of a reward.*

This is a proven fact not only among adult humans, but also among children, and even among young animals.

People perform the worst and will usually always fail and rebel when given only the threat of punishment.

Ask the best of animal trainers, even those who train lions and tigers.

They use the promise of reward more than the threat of punishment.

Even to reform the worst of rapists, this is sometimes true.

But I always believe before the promise of reward, one must bear punishment for their actions especially if it is wicked actions that caused the suffering of another innocent person.

- *Never assume things, ASSUME just makes and ASS of U and ME.*

Before arriving at a conclusion, depending on the answer you want, first always ask the questions:

- *"Let me know what you think first?"*
- *"Why did you say that?"*
- *"What do you mean?"*

- *Consider the cumulative effect, not the recency effect.*

Most of us only consider the last interaction in a relationship.

Even if a person has been good to us previously, even for decades, but did something hurtful recently, we forget all the past good things and can even breakup a multi-decade relationship just because of the most recent bad experience.

Relationships once broken cannot be restored.

Work hard at saving a long-term relationship.

When the relationship is down to its last threads, then work even more hard at saving even the last thread of that relationship.

Even if you have to cut off the thread of a new or unstable relationship, to save a valuable long-term relationship, do it without hesitation.

Some people say that a broken relationship can be restored.

This is not true.

A good relationship is like a strong steel ropes of a wire bridge.

It is extremely valuable until the last thread breaks.

Once that thread is broken, there is only disaster and loss that follows.

A good relationship is also like a clear unbroken unscratched beautiful mirror.

It is clear and beautiful, and you love to look at it all the time since it unconditionally reflects all your actions and makes you look and feel good and laughs and cries with you.

Once the mirror is broken it shatters into pieces.

The clear unblemished reflection is permanently lost.

Even if all the pieces are gathered and pasted together, the cracks will still remain visible and you will never get the original unblemished reflection of a clear unbroken mirror.

There are only two things left to do with a broken mirror:

- Remain satisfied with a broken mirror whose clear reflection you will never regain or enjoy again.
- Discard the old mirror and get a new mirror whose reflection you will again enjoy.

Money can buy many things, but cannot restore a destroyed relationship nor restore a broken mirror.

However, this also has exceptions: Even if a person has been good to you in the past, but is continuously harmful and hurtful to you in the recent past for at least three years or more, then it is better to review the relationship from a futuristic perspective and make your decision considering your future wellbeing.

There is a golden saying in the Mutual Fund and Hedge Fund and other Investment Fund industries which are the biggest ever con games devised by the Wall Street/Dalal Street Pimps:

"Past performance is no guarantee of future results."

- *Do not value relationships more than religion.*

If you have to have to let go of religion to save a relationship, do that without any second thought.

- *In fact, do not value relationships more than monetary considerations or anything material.*
- *But be willing to sacrifice all relationships to protect Dharma.*
- *Have long term relationships.*

Long term relationships in business or personal affairs are stable, and stability brings trust and that is a good thing.

Never forget your oldest and your childhood friends.

They are the only ones who were friends with you for who you were, not what you may have become later in life.

Old friends are like gold.

One popular saying:

Make new friends, but don't forget the old,

One is silver, the other is gold.

Another popular saying:

Old friends are gold! New friends are diamonds!

If you get diamonds, don't forget gold,

Because diamonds can only be set in gold.

- *If you give in plenty first, you will get a lot more than you have given.*

Give a person respect the first time you meet them.

Give equal respect to any person, from the manhole cleaner to the supreme leader.

Give a person kindness the first time you meet them.

Give a person compassion the first time you meet them.

- *The most ignorant and stupid saying is "Evil prevails when good men are silent and do nothing".*

Good men would not be silent if they saw evil prevailing.

Evil prevails because selfish evil men tolerate other evil men doing selfish evil things to other people.

Selfish evil men remain silent because the other evil men are not doing evil things to their family or their loved ones but to someone else's family and loved ones.

If these other evil men had done evil things to this selfish person's family, they would have been the first to rise up and stop the other evil men.

And as I have said before:

Selfishness is the root cause of all evil.

In my opinion, Bhishma was one of the most remarkable men ever in the history of the world.

He would have been on the same level of Lord Ram, if he had only placed adherence to Dharma above adherence to his family.

Bhishma thought he was following Dharma by honouring his promise to his father, but he was also one of its greatest violators.

He was blind to the faults of his family.

He was not only blind, but also silent about their faults and even condoned it when they continuously committed the most grievous violations Dharma, including the public molestation of a woman who was also a wife, mother and his close relative almost akin to a granddaughter.

One cannot remain blind and silent and condone any violations of Dharma, even if they are your done by your own family.

If you remain silent about evil, you are no better than the evil doer.

That is why Lord Ram is remembered with reverence even to this day: *He put adherence to Dharma not only above himself, but also above the wellbeing of his most beloved pregnant wife and unborn child.*

Lord Ram loved Sita more than himself.

Yet he sacrificed her and his unborn child because of Dharma.

One has to understand the conditions of those days to understand what Lord Ram did.

Considering today's times, where serial adulterer and sexual predator Pompous Prick presidents, can have a nude supermodel third wife as First Lady of USA, some people are misguided and think what Lord Ram did was harsh and unfair and unreasonable.

But it is a really complex issue to understand Lord Ram's plight and what led to his painful decision to hurt his most beloved wife and unborn child.

- *Another of the most ignorant and stupid sayings is "Everything is fair in love and war".*

Nothing is fair if Dharma is violated. But everything is fair to protect Dharma.

- *Hate the sin, not the sinner.*

Do not condemn the person entirely, but only condemn and punish the bad quality in that person until it is removed and they reform.

Read my articles on Justice and Punishment to understand more about this.

- *Do not worry about your reputation, but always focus on your character every moment you breathe.*

If you have a good character, your reputation will come automatically without any additional effort.

Be good in your thoughts first, only then can you develop character.

What you think is what you speak and what you will do.

- *Reputation is what others think of you. Character is what you think of yourself.*

Today most people are more bothered about developing their reputation than their character.

They measure their success not by the strength of their character, but the strength of their material wealth, even if this wealth has been procured through petty and dishonest means.

Even if they are third class porkis in their character and behaviour, they are not bothered about reforming their character, they just want to develop an appearance of being gentlemen so that they can get a good reputation.

They develop this reputation by "donating" a small amount of their immense wealth to so called "charitable" purposes, that are actually just business and self-promotion expenses towards enhancing their so called "reputation" as gentlemen.

They appear to meeker than a mouse and more polite to people from whom they are expecting some gain or benefit.

They also appear to meeker than a mouse and more polite to people who can bully them or could defame them or damage their reputation

But they will more wicked than a rabid dog to people who they think they can bully and from who they have nothing to gain from and think cannot affect their reputation.

A person may openly violate Dharma and even question the existence of Brahman, but if they "donate" a few lakhs to a so called "temple" they will be given a status higher than the most ardent and sincere devotee.

Unfortunately as is already written in the Shrimad Bhagavatam, Ramacharit Manas, Brighu and other texts about the evils of the Kaliyuga:

In the Kaliyuga, people are measured by the strength of their wealth not by the strength of their character.

- *Do not worry about success but strive to achieve satisfaction.*

Success is a measure of your efforts by others, satisfaction is a measure of your efforts by yourself.

- *The most important and priceless asset of yours is not your health, but your time.*

If you manage your time well, you can easily manage your life and even your health which is the next important asset after time.

Time is the most precious commodity and treats all equally, the poorest of the poor or even the richest billionaires.

You cannot recover time when it is lost even if you are willing to pay a hundred trillion dollars for it.

Proper time management is very important to have a healthy and happy life.

Divide your time with a proper allocation for family, rest, exercise, ध्यान (Dhyan) and food.

Once all this is in balance, then your time at work will automatically be the most productive even if it is short.

Life is much more than just working to earn a living.

The end goal of your life should not be only your work.

A day will come when you will no longer be working and forced to stop working – either you may get old, or tired or fired.

There is a golden saying:

Love your job, not your company, because you never know when your company may stop loving you.

But the other components of your life – family, rest, exercise, meditation, and food remain with you and love you dearly till the end of your life and are the main contributors to your wellbeing.

Treat time as your most precious asset.

Be very careful how you spend your time. Especially when you spend it on people.

Spend your time only on your True Family, who will value and be grateful for the time you have spent for them, even if you have not given them anything material.

For the rest of the people just give them material things or money.

Most times we end up wasting time on people who do not really value our time, but actually only value our money.

- *Be a Finder, not a Seeker.*

A seeker is looking for something, they are so caught up looking for that one single thing, that they forget the pleasures of the journey itself.

Be a finder, like a child on a picnic in a forest.

Have no goal, instead be free and open.

Be open to receive even the smallest of wonders that life sends you, even the simplest of things like the flight of a butterfly or the falling of raindrops.

Let things discover you, don't go out trying to discover things.

Only finders discover happiness, seekers are always frustrated pursuing and looking for the next big high.

As Jiddu said: "*Happiness is not a thing to be pursued; it comes.*

But if you seek it, it will evade you."

- *Always be polite and respectful and start off being nice.*

I have made more friends than enemies and that is how I always start off any relationship.

- *Always try to have a discussion, not an argument.*

A discussion: A polite and civil exchange of enlightened knowledge and ideas without ego and anger and acceptance of an enlightened view even if it is contrary to your own.

An argument: A violent exchange of ignorance, anger, and ego by dumbasses.

- *Always forget what you give, but never forget to forgive.*

I got the above wonderful saying from this wonderful Youtube video: https://youtu.be/7qgd_vxgeh4

- *It is the thought and devotion that counts, not the value of the gift.*

Some people think only people who give them really expensive gifts really care for them. They also think the only way that they can show they care for a person is to buy an expensive gift for that person.

As Jiddu said:

```
Now  you  have  the  mind  full  and  your  heart
empty.
```

Value people according to the thought and dedication they put into the gift. Rich people may send their drivers to buy an expensive Rs 500 greeting card with pre-written fancy words from a fancy store, but a poor person who puts his heart and soul into the greeting even if he writes in pencil on a cheap ordinary piece of paper and with a lot of spelling mistakes, it has more value than a careless pre-written fancy greeting card.

As Lord Krishna said in the Gita:

```
If  one  offers  Me  with  love  and  devotion  a
leaf, a flower, fruit, or water, I will accept
it.
```

Chapter 9 (Raja Yoga), Verse 26

- *You never know what you can get until you ask for it.*
- *You can never know another's suffering unless you go through the same suffering yourself.*

- *A good way to start a conversation with a stranger is to ask the question "Where are you from? "and then "What do you do?"*
- *Have an open mind – Learn to listen and listen to learn.*

A mind that is closed and has preconceived and rigid notions is a mind that is closed, and anything closed does not have room to grow and flourish.

A closed mind is like dark and stuffy room where there is no light and fresh air, it is absolutely not a comfortable place to be.

As Leo Tolstoy said:

The most difficult subjects can be explained to the most slow-witted man if he has not formed any idea of them already; but the simplest thing cannot be made clear to the most intelligent man if he is firmly persuaded that he knows already, without a shadow of doubt, what is laid before him.

- *Clarity of purpose beats force of will any day.*

When you have clarity of purpose, you will automatically find a way that is sure and simple.

The saying *"Where there is a will, there is a way"* is a stupid saying devised by a world class dumbass.

It is like taking a hammer to get through a brick wall when you can just look around the corner and find the door and get behind the wall with much less time and effort.

First develop clarity of purpose, then the way will automatically unfold in front of you.

- *To be a success at work or at anything material, do things because you want to do it, not because you have to do it.*

When you work on something because you *want to do it,* you don't need to be motivated.

You will do it wholeheartedly and with full devotion.

Whenever you do something wholeheartedly and with full devotion it is usually a success as long as you have *clarity of purpose.*

- *But to be a success at life and achieve Moksha, for the protection of Dharma, do things because you have to do it, even if you don't want to do it.*

- *Do everything with devotion not dedication.*

Being dedicated is going to work and sincerely doing your duty.

Being devoted is like going to a temple, or for the more enlightened, practicing ध्यान (Dhyan) and offering SEVA to Nature and the True Temples.

There is no expectation of a reward, just the joy of the action.

Devotion is doing it for love, dedication is doing it for duty.

- *Working with devotion is useless without discipline and perseverance.*

Discipline and perseverance (grit) are the keys for any achievement in life.

A person may have focus, clarity of purpose, force of will and devotion.

But without discipline and perseverance(grit), everything is useless.

What exactly is perseverance(grit)?

Like the boxing saying goes:

Take a licking but keep on ticking.

Grit means never giving up even after failing and being knocked down.

What exactly is discipline?

Discipline starts by first being willing to accept responsibility for one's actions.

Only a person who is willing to be responsible, is capable of being disciplined.

Our fraud education system thinks that caning and threat of punishment will inculcate a sense of discipline.

Discipline cannot be inculcated by punishment.

It has to be inculcated by motivating the heart and cheering and enlightening the spirit.

The Army is the paradigm of discipline.

Some people may say that the army inculcates discipline by harsh methods and threat of punishment.

This is not completely true.

The Army inculcates discipline by developing the ultimate sense of SEVA in a solider – a sense of responsibility for the wellbeing of the nation.

Hence developing a sense of SEVA in a person will automatically inculcate discipline.

Some may say that SEVA is a too philosophical term and why do I always bring the concept of SEVA to all my writing.

There is a saying:

Charity begins at home.

So first inculcate a sense of SEVA towards your own wellbeing.

Only a person who can take care of themselves first, is truly capable of taking care of others.

- *Don't ever be selfish or unreasonable or unwilling to compromise.*

- *Wealth is important, but not everything.*

It is good to have money, but money alone will not make a person happy.

Instead of being unhappy in a one room thatched leaking house, you may be unhappy in a marble floored bungalow, but the fact remains you are still unhappy.

- *Don't love and respect monetarily rich persons, but love and respect good persons.*

Ram, Jesus, Buddha, Ramakrishna and Swami Vivekanand were not the monetarily richest men of their times.

But they remain the richest men, even after millenniums, for they remain in our hearts and we value them for their goodness and character and the examples they set of themselves for humanity to follow.

Can you name even one of the monetarily richest men of those times?

- *Empathy and generosity of heart is much more valuable than generosity of money.*

True generosity is if you are willing to sacrifice your most cherished and valued efforts for the benefit of somebody else without any expectations.

And more importantly if you are willing to let that person take the benefit of your efforts and give them the free will and choice to let them grow and direct the progress of your gift to them.

Even if you are pauper but have the above generosity of heart, you are much richer than any billionaire who can only give paper money, that too only after they die and that too only for "charitable" purposes that they propose and specify in their will which is mainly for the sole purpose of furthering their legacy and for the own self-interest.

- *Do not judge a book by its cover.*

The only way to judge a book is by reading the content of every chapter to the entire end of the book.

That is the same way to judge a person: *By reading the content of their character and the sum of their actions, not just the content of their external appearance or most recent actions.*

A person's external appearance is just like the cover page of a book.

Their character and sum of their actions are the true indicator of their worth.

We must never judge a person based on preconceived notions or assumptions based on their appearance, gender, religious, economic, or social background.

Many times, almost 99.99999% of the time, the most remarkable of people are found only when you take the trouble to bother to remove the apparent veil over their appearance.

The veil should be removed from your eyes, it is your veil of ignorance which is blinding your vision.

Their appearance is as radiant and beautiful as it always ways, it is just covered by your veil of ignorance.

There is a saying that is absolutely true:

What you see in others is a true reflection of what you actually are yourself.

Never care about people who only judge you by your wealth or appearance or ancestry.

They will be the first to abandon you when you lose the above.

Always care about people who have a rich heart.

They care about you, not your wealth or appearance or ancestry.

- *A rich heart may be under a poor coat.*

This is wonderful video below from which I got the above saying:

https://youtu.be/q6ZUfc9R-eg

- *Do not judge beauty only by good looks.*

Mother   Teresa, Ramakrishna, Sharada   Mata, Swami Vivekanand were beautiful human beings, though they may not have been as good looking as our eye candy supermodels and movie stars.

This world is fooled by appearances and material illusions like wealth, dynasty, fame, good looks, rituals, public prayer, big talk, flattery, false claims, false promises and the arrogance of title and power.

It does even pause to consider and realise the true value of actual wisdom, character, and a sense of Dharma in not just words, but also in thought and action.

As Jiddu said:

Outward beauty can never last, it is marred always if there is no inward delight and joy.

We cultivate the outer, paying so little attention to the thing inside the skin; but it is the inner that always overcomes the outer.

It is the worm inside the apple that destroys the freshness of the apple.

- *The true character of a person is known only when you give them wealth and power.*

If you really want to know the true character of a person, give them wealth and power, and then ask the employees and associates junior and subordinate to the person about their interaction with that person.

Especially the most junior level of his employees and associates from who he feels he has nothing to gain like the cleaner, teaboy, driver, and office boy.

If you don't work with the person, then go out with them to the cheapest restaurant and see how they treat the waiter and table cleaner.

- *You cannot have a split personality – there is no separate business and personal character.*

There is only one character and it shows both in business and personal affairs.

- *Your true friends, relatives and well-wishers are known only when you have lost all your wealth and power.*

- *Actions speak louder than words.*

There is a saying:

"Empty vessels make the most noise".

Never trust a person who flatters you and uses sweet words and swears undying loyalty to you.

Never count on a person who boasts and talks big, to do any task of importance.

The person who you should trust the most is the one who walks into your life and stands by you in the worst of times.

A person who is genuinely happy for your joys and truly sorry for your sorrows.

Such people don't make a show of such things in big flowery words or big actions like cheering and clapping.

It is usually in small gestures of warm hugs and silent but brilliant smiles of joy, and silent but painful tears of sorrow.

- *Empty Vessels make the most noise.*

Never take a person who talks big of himself seriously.

Unfortunately most of our Representative DFIs, including our NRI Business Development Manager, his chaddi dost Obama and also the Pompous Prick in the USA, come to power because the public thinks they are "Brilliant Orators".

There is no difference between a "Brilliant Orator" and a "Smooth Talker".

The end result of both is to impress people by their words and not their actions.

A "Brilliant Orator" is like a loud fart: First all you hear is the loud noise and you even laugh and even joke about it, and some even are proud of it.

Only later do you realise the stinky smell of shit which causes embarrassment and discomfort not only to the farter but mainly to the others also in the same room.

There is no difference between a "Brilliant Orator" and an asshole.

Finally all that comes out of them is stinky shit.

- *Still Waters run Deep.*

This is a really brilliant saying in the English language.

It means a person who has deep character, knowledge, experience, and wisdom, will usually be humble and quiet and let their achievements speak for themselves.

They will not foolishly promote themselves by making loud verbal diarrhoea farts with their "Brilliant Oratory".

- *Never sacrifice your self-respect or principles for money.*

As they say:

"A man for whom money is everything, will do anything for money."

- *Poverty is the worst of crimes against humanity.*

As the Shanthi Parva says, to be poor is to be cursed.

A person in poverty only thinks about survival and getting their next meal and not going hungry.

There is even a story in the Upanishads, about a learned Vedic scholar who could recite all the Vedas by heart, but completely forgot all the Vedas when he went hungry.

The poor do not even dream about living or being spiritual or trying to inquire into the higher ideals of life.

Poverty also sometimes makes a person desperate and a desperate person does wicked actions.

How would one define poor?

I would say that one is poor if one does not have access primarily to food, water, health care, education, accommodation, justice, rule of law, and security.

Once we develop these basic things, in the next step we can then also add telephone and internet communication and public transport.

- *Go to school and get a true education at least till 3rd form (8th Standard).*

I do not remember most of what I was taught in school, but the memories of the friends I made, and the joy I brought to my parents when I did well at school and when I graduated from college will always remain.

It also did help me get my job.

I did learn things in school that did have applications in my job too.

Some of the smartest people I know only had a 3rd form (8th Standard) education.

They knew how to read, write, and count and used it in varied ways with a very open and flexible mind.

And they did much better than many PhD graduates.

They even raised children who went on to become Generals, Doctors, Lawyers, and world class businessmen.

In Bharat, especially in these times, only those who study in English medium are considered to be "educated".

A person who studies in English medium, can only be considered English literate.

Most likely, fit only to be a qualified candidate to write job exams in English.

True education is only attained when one becomes a decent human being.

- *Don't work just to make money and get rich.*

You will never be successful, nor make any money, if you work only to make money and get rich.

Develop a talent and work hard, smart, persistently, patiently, and devotedly to perfect that talent.

Work to achieve extreme expertise and competence in that talent.

Once you develop extreme expertise at your talent, you will automatically be successful.

All that follows your success, like money and fame is just because of your extreme expertise in the talent you have.

Money and fame are not end results in themselves.

They are by-products for the success you have achieved at perfecting your talent and this can only come from vision, devoted, sustained hard and smart work.

- *Remember it is smart work that counts, not hard work.*

The donkeys are the hardest working animals, but the man who rides the donkey cart is the smartest worker.

Even though he is just one man, he can get a hundred donkeys to work for him, and even though he is not doing as much physical work as the donkeys, the success of the donkeys' journey depends on him.

His success lies in the fact that he knows the road ahead and where it will lead while the donkeys just concentrate on the potholes in front of them.

Because the donkeys are just looking at the potholes on the road, and not where the road leads, they may end up on a one way road that leads off a cliff.

- *To be truly happy and successful you must follow your talents, not passion or monetary incentives as your main vocation.*

Choosing a job just for the sake of a good salary is the biggest lie that you are telling yourself.

Just because you have a passion for something does not mean you are good at it.

Everybody has a passion to be a musician, actor, dancer, or painter, but very few have any real talent for it.

Find your talent, everybody has some gift that they are really good at.

What is talent?

It is doing something really well that comes naturally to you, without any additional effort but others find difficult to do and even admire you for your ability to do it.

Remember even talent has to be developed.

Develop your talent with regular practice, devotion, perseverance, and hard and smart work.

Once you are really good at it, it will automatically make a living for you.

Some people say that if you have a passion for something and work hard at it, you will surely work wonders.

I do not think that this is true, there has to be some basic level of talent first.

You cannot make a crystal glass from pure sand alone.

No matter how much you try, some amount of lead has to be added to make crystal glass.

Talent is that "lead", you must have it to make crystal.

Without talent (lead), you will only have ordinary glass, no matter if you use the same technique to manufacture crystal glass a thousand times.

However lead will always remain lead, if it is not mixed with sand and then made to undergo the melting heat and the rest of the arduous process to be manufactured into crystal.

Hence a talent is useless unless it is developed, and that is possible only by practice, devotion, persistence, and smart work.

- *Triumph only comes through trials.*

Anybody who boasts that they have never failed, has not tasted true success at all.

Only a person who has tasted failure, knows how to succeed.

Anybody who boasts that they have achieved things easily without much effort have not tasted true success at all.

Only a person who has recovered from failure, and not only worked hard, but also worked smart and with clarity of purpose has tasted true success.

Triumph only comes through trials.

- *Have compassion and be charitable in thought, word, and deed.*
- *Do not wish for things to happen, do something to make it happen.*
- *Destiny is what you make of it, but your Karma is in your hands like the potter's mould, and Brahman dispassionately turns the wheel of the Rtam.*

Remember you are responsible for your Karma.

Just like a potter's mould, your Karma is mainly is in your hands.

But like the potter's wheel, Brahman is responsible of turning of the wheel, for the absolutely dispassionate dispensation of the Rtam.

The Rtam just keeps turning like the potter's wheel, it does not care what you make of your Karma.

If you have good Karma you will have a beautiful pot, if you have bad Karma you will have a wrangled mess of clay.

If you have bad Karma, you have to start all over again with that wrangled mess of clay.

- *A man cannot directly choose his circumstances, but he can choose his thoughts, and so indirectly, yet surely, shape his circumstances.*

This is a wonderful saying by James Allen.

- *Only losers complain about problems, winners provide solutions to problems.*
- *Use moderation in everything you do.*

Even a little drinking or gambling is fine.

As long as it is done in moderation and not in excess.

Anything done in excess, not only drinking and gambling, but even being excessively loving and kind to somebody, finally only brings ruin to a person.

- *Do hate anything or anyone, just ignore and forget about them.*

Ignoring and indifference is much more hurting to a person than hating them.

Get these people you don't like out of your mind.

Don't even think about them.

As Swami Vivekanand said:

I gain whether you love or hate me,

If you love me, I am in your heart,

If you hate me, I am in your mind.

- *Do not hate or fear the unknown.*

- *Do not hate or prejudge any group of people you don't know personally at an individual level.*

It is wrong to hate all Muslims or Blacks or Mexicans or Pakistanis.

There are many Arya and Brahma Dana among them.

- *Do not love or prejudge any group of people you do not know personally at an individual level.*

It is wrong to like all Whites, or Hindus or Jews.

There are many Anarya and Wicked among them.

- *Make fun of the government and people in authority, always be cynical about them and always verify their motives and expose any hypocrisy.*

- *Do not make fun of a person's God, family, friends or some achievements they are proud of.*

Some people will fight you bitterly for this even and destroy decades long relationships, even if you know them really well.

- *If you don't think about women as sex objects or don't think that you are better than them, you will have more women friends and associates.*

- *Only make promises you can keep otherwise just say no.*

- *Do not fight with violence (forcefully) unless you have exhausted all other options and absolutely have no other option.*

According to the Sanathan Dharma there are four stages of fighting:

- Sama (try to befriend or form alliance)
- Dana (give gifts, presents, and do favours)
- Bheda (confuse, deceive, separate, divide and rule)
- And finally when all else fails Dhand (military or physical force).

- *Be fearless but also pragmatic and realise that discretion is the better part of valour.*

Some of the greatest battles were won by people who were not only fearless but also had discretion and knew when to retreat when faced with losses, then regrouped and came back much stronger.

Remember the saying:

He who fights and runs away, lives to fight another day.

Some people may think I am talking like this since I am basically a coward.

I also used to think like the rest of the so called brave but actually foolhardy people:

Stand to the last man.

Sometimes I have taken the most foolish risks standing alone unarmed against a bunch of uncouth lecherous rowdies.

But by the grace of Brahman, I was blessed to have not a hair touched on my head by rowdies, because the crowd who faced me were basically cowards.

So they just walked away when faced with my resistance and threat of much worse to happen to them than what they would do to me.

I have also wandered in gang violence prone areas in the USA counting only on the protection of Brahman, who of course did protect me since I am still standing unharmed today.

What I believe is sometimes true:

Sometimes all it takes it one brave heart to strike fear in millions of cowards.

You will notice I said "sometimes".

There are always many exceptions to the above rule and my idealism also got tempered by harsh reality when I read the advice of Bhishma in the Shanti Parva.

I don't remember the exact words, but it was something on the lines of:

`When in extreme danger and all is lost, save`
`yourself at all costs.`

You can regain everything you lost and help everybody who depend on you, if you save yourself.

If you lose yourself, everything you have is lost, and your family is left to the wilderness.

There can be no braver man and greater general than Bhishma.

So what I say has the backing of one of the greatest warriors and generals in the history of the world.

- *Value True Moral Courage more than Physical Courage.*

"Common experience shows how much rarer is moral courage than physical bravery.

A thousand men will march to the mouth of the cannon where one man will dare espouse an unpopular cause . . . True courage and manhood come from the consciousness of the right attitude toward the world, the faith in one's purpose, and the sufficiency of one's own approval as a justification for one's own acts."

Clarence Darrow, Resist Not Evil

"The man who can face vilification and disgrace, who can stand up against the popular current, even against his friends and his country when he know he is right, who can defy those in authority over him, who can take punishment and prison and remain steadfast-that is a man of courage.

The fellow whom you taunt as a 'slacker' because he refuses to turn murderer-he needs courage.

But do you need much courage just to obey orders, to do as you are told and to fall in line with thousands of others to the tune of general approval and the Star Spangled Banner?"

Alexander Berkman

- *Speak out your mind and fear no one.*

At the same time, even if you speak out your mind, try to put it the most kind, gentle and non-humiliating words possible.

An iron hand behind a velvet glove, has a much better effect than whipping somebody and humiliating them in public.

- *Live within your means and never borrow more than you can pay back.*
- *In fact it would be best if you do not borrow at all.*

Live simply, save your earnings and then buy things you really need, not things that you want.

- *Learn from the past, but do not dwell on the bad things that happened in the past.*
- *Live for today, like it is your last day in this world.*
- *Plan for tomorrow, but do not worry about it.*
- *Read and practice the primary teachings (Vedanta, Bhagavada Gita and if possible Brahmasutra) of the Sanathan Dharma especially and also the Sakyamuni.*

- *Be happy with what you have especially if you have enough.*

- *Learn to let go gracefully.*

When the times comes for you to leave this world, make all preparations with complete transparency and the full consent of your successors.

Otherwise, all that you have built will only end in disputes, destruction, abandonment, and ruin.

Let go gracefully while you are still alive. Do not wait for God to take things from you without your consent.

- *Leave enough for needs, not for wants.*

Those of us who are fortunate and have earned enough wealth must leave at least 50% of our wealth to our family.

But do not give them so much that they lead an idle and wasteful existence.

Given them enough for their needs and for a decent living so that they have the freedom to practice their talents and passions.

Give them enough so that they do not have to be forced to do work they don't like just for the sake of earning money.

But they still have to work because they like what they are doing.

But do not give them so much that they waste their time in idleness and wasteful desires.

If they want more than they need, let them earn it themselves.

- *It helps to take risks, but only risk what you can afford to lose.*
- *Never give up, always be persistent and patient.*

Remember even if you get sour grapes, be patient, leave them to dry and you will get raisins which are much more sweeter and even more profitable than fresh grapes.

- *Think big – aim for the stars.*

Then at least you will reach the mango tree.

- *Always look at the big picture first, then work out the details.*

I was trained as a Civil Engineer, so that is the fundamental rule of surveying:

From Whole to Part.

- *But remember the big picture can only be drawn with attention to fine details.*
- *Document what is most precious to you.*

Don't just talk, memory can fail, and you can forget precious moments, and you cannot share memories with your loved ones. Take photos, videos, audios, write letters and emails.

- *Do not watch the Presstitutes TV News.*

Instead read good independent newspapers and independent websites.

In fact many newspapers also today are Presstitutes.

TV News from the Presstitutes is for people who are ignorant and lazy and don't want to think and find out for themselves.

The only option left is some independent reputed newspapers, independent news websites and reputed blogs on the internet.

Never get your news from Whatsapp and Facebook. It is highly unreliable.

- *Watch very little TV and do not have a cable TV connection.*

Watching TV really does rot your brain and make you a dumbass.

There are many reputed scientific studies that have proven that TV really does rot your brain especially in young children who watch TV.

Watching TV leads to antisocial behaviour, lowered verbal IQ, obesity, diabetes, and mental health problems because of altered brain structure.

- *Develop a good and consistent reading habit.*

Develop a good and consistent reading habit right from childhood.

Read a wide variety of material – from comics to novels to spiritual stuff to anything that really interests you.

Now with the advent of the Internet the whole worlds library is available on your computer or tablet or even mobile, a major part of it for free, even from the world's leading universities like MIT and Harvard and IIT.

There is even Google Translator so you can reasonably translate foreign material also.

It may not be the perfect translation, but it gives you a decent idea of the material.

- *Try to be an intellectual but definitely be an expert at something.*

An intellectual is someone who knows a little about a lot of things and knows where to find experts.

An expert is someone who knows more and more about less and less.

The prophecy of the advent of the Satyuga

Bhudevi is Mother Earth.

Bhudevi was the wife of Varaha.

When Bhudevi was in trouble, Narayana(Vishnu) took the avatar of Varaha to save Bhudevi from Hiranyaksha.

Sita was the daughter of Bhudevi. Sita was also the wife of Rama.

When Sita was in trouble, Narayana(Vishnu) took the avatar of Rama to save her from Ravana.

Sita was the epitome of womanhood.

Yet Rama banished and abandoned her.

When a husband abandons his wife, the only option left for her solace is her mother.

So Sita, the epitome of womanhood, prayed to Bhudevi:

If never in thought and word and deed I have permitted myself even in a dream to dwell on any person other than my lord (Rama), then O Mother Bhudevi, listen, let me abide in your lap.

The moment Sita uttered these words, a deafening sound was heard and the earth opened up. Then an impeccably beauteous throne appeared, borne by the thousand-

headed Sheshanag, and Bhudevi, the redeemer of the world was seated incarnate upon it.

At once, she took Janaki (Sita) into her lap and admonishing, blessed her and Bhudevi and said:

You have daughter, suffered greatly; now come and enjoy the blessings available in my realm.

With due courtesy, Bhudevi set Sita upon the bejewelled throne, which vanished into the nether world - a glorious marvel beyond words;

Lakshmana and others were utterly dumbfounded at this marvel, their eyes streaming with tears.

Having witnessed all this, the all-gracious Lord realised that Sita had a premonition of his return to his own (Saket, Vaikunta).

Hiranyaksha and Ravana were extremely powerful Rakshasas or the worst and most Wicked of demons.

But they could be easily defeated because they were just two demons.

Hiranyaksha and Ravana may have been extremely powerful enough to destroy armies of the mightiest of Gods.

But still they were just two demons and so Brahman just took the form of Vishnu, a part of Narayana to destroy them.

In the age of Kuly (the demon, not the Goddess), the Kaliyuga, Kuly (the demon) enters the hearts of billions of people who are Anarya (fools).

Due to the "wonder" of FUKUS "democracy" and capitalism, even SAT (Truth), the last and most fundamental leg of Dharma, is being destroyed.

Due to the "wonder" of FUKUS "democracy", Anarya (fools) elect millions of Dhushta (Wicked) Representative DFIs as their leaders because they are fooled by "Brilliant Oratory" and smart marketing and paid pimping by the Presstitutes.

Due to the "wonder" of FUKUS capitalism, Anarya (fools) work as bonded debt ridden slaves for Dhushta (Wicked) Wall Street/Dalal Street Pimps and Lalas as their leaders because they are fooled by brilliant marketing scam of Globalisation and the "wonder" of FUKUS capitalism.

In age of Kuly (the demon), everything is at risk – Bhudevi (Mother Earth), Sita (women) and even two year old children.

In age of Kuly (the demon), the highest Yoga is Bhakti.

In age of Kuly (the demon), Dharma is on its last leg.

Dharma may be on its last leg, but Dharma will never be destroyed.

Dharma cannot be destroyed.

It is the supreme law created by Brahman and above all so called "laws" of man.

Dharma defends those who defend it.

And Dharma destroys those who destroy it.

This is the ultimate teaching of the Sanathan Dharma.

When Dharma is down to its last leg, Brahman itself comes down to defend it.

Who is Brahman?

तत् त्वम् असि *Tat Tvam Asi – That is the Truth, That is the Self, That You Are.*

YOU ARE BRAHMAN.

The whole of Bharat is Brahman, not just the people of Bharat.

Together we all form ब्रह्मन् Brahman.

But ब्रह्मन् Brahman is also Shakti, Brahma, Narayana and Rudra and all the Gods of the Vedas.

Shakti is the mother of all creation.

Brahma is the creator of the Multiverse.

Narayana is the sustainer of the Multiverse.

Rudra is the destroyer of the Multiverse.

The Gods of the Vedas have their own powers.

The whole of Bharat has suffered for more than the last three hundred years under FUKUS and more recently under its cursed systems of "democracy" and "capitalism".

Bharat takes pride to be ruled by FUKUS systems of the "rule of law".

FUKUS proudly establishes itself as the bastion of the "rule of law".

But the law in FUKUS is made by liars and thieves.

The whole foundation for wealth and power in FUKUS systems are based on lying and thieving.

Lying for power, by the Representative DFIs.

Thieving for wealth, by both the Representative DFIs and the Wall Street/Dalal Street Pimps and Lalas.

For Bharat and this world to regain its wellbeing and its historical fame and contentment, it must burn the fraud FUKUS systems, just like FUKUS will be burned along with its systems.

Rudra has already started putting this message into a real sword by subjecting the USA, the main king of FUKUS and the so called bastion of "democracy" and "capitalism" into fury and vengeance that will be unrivalled in the history of this world.

2019 will be a landmark year for the USA.

The end of its beginning and the beginning of its end.

Fire and floods have started.

Winds will freeze and then burn and then blow away everything in its path.

Waters will freeze and melt and flood and wash away everything in its path causing famine.

Drought will then follow causing more famine and social unrest.

And finally the earth will explode in an earth shattering manner, laying waste to whatever FUKUS foolishly thought they could do to conquer Nature.

Then the currency will collapse, and prices will rise by the minute.

Of course it goes without saying, that the Pompous Prick and Dumbass Dubya will be eliminated in a spectacular fashion.

And then the USA will be a living embodiment of the story of the Lord of the Flies.

And this will continue until the One returns to the USA.

That means a minimum of 25 years (mid 2040s).

Considering that the USA has spread its grand vision of the Lord of the Flies to various parts of the world, including to its own original native born citizens, for more than 250 years, 25 years of payback is just a minor technicality.

Bharat was always renowned for the rule of Dharma and only gained contentment for millenniums only by following the rule of Dharma.

Bharat must return to the rule of Dharma.

And the rule of Dharma is divine rule by Brahman.

The website www.aryadharma.world is the horse of Brahman.

The message on this website is the sword of Rudra and chakra of Narayana.

It transports the wheel of Dharma.

And I have already explained who Brahman is.

The whole of Bharat is Brahman, not just the people of Bharat.

Narayana always comes down as an avatar in human form.

In the age of the Satyuga, the Raja (Highest) Yoga is ध्यान Dhyan or Dhyana.

You will see ध्यान (Dhyan) in Bharat.

Not just as a man, but as an ideal.

Not just in one man, but in the whole of Bharat.

You will hear about ध्यान (Dhyan) in FUKUS.

What government and presstitutes talk about ध्यान (Dhyan) is what will happen to them because that is what they did to ध्यान (Dhyan).

And what is done in FUKUS and all countries that harmed Bharat will be done by Rudra and by the people of those countries themselves.

The prophecy of Nostradamus:

Quatrain 2,28

French
Le penultiesme du surnom du Prophete,
Prendra Diane pour son iour & repos:
Loing vaguera par frenetique teste,
En deliurant vn grand peuple d'impos.

English
God the Last but First (the seer)
Takes Dhyan, for his Day & Movement
He will wander far because of a frantic head,
And delivering a great people from subjection.

For more detailed prophecies from Nostradamus refer to the Angel of the Moon (https://bit.ly/2lwI5pE).

It is written in the Brahmasutra and Gita and Yoga Vasistha:

Only those who follow ध्यान (Dhyan) will reach ब्रह्मन् (Brahman).

Following ध्यान (Dhyan) does not mean just following a man named Dhyan.

Following ध्यान (Dhyan) means practicing ध्यान (Dhyan) in every thought and action of yours to become a Yogi who has achieved समत्वम् (Samathvam).

For the Satyuga to return, you must follow ध्यान (Dhyan) not just in name but always mainly in practice.

NOTE:

On March 12, 2003 I had what I think was a divine revelation.

I call it a vision.

In a fraction of a second, I saw the next 40 years of not only my life, but the entire world until the adulthood of my son.

Because of the importance of that vision, I was overwhelmed with happiness.

I was shouting to the world about the vision, that I was the messenger and I must be taken to the supreme leader and that there would be hell to pay in the land of Abraham and the USA if I was not taken seriously and the supreme leader (President Bush) still went ahead with the war in Iraq which was yet to begin and God and sent me as the messenger to prevent.

I have never felt such happiness, fright, and excitement ever in my life.

Already almost 20 years of the fright I saw has come true.

My revelations about the destruction of the USA are coming true and you have already seen this happening in the land of Abraham (the Middle East) which will end with the destruction of the land of Abraham (Israel).

The hell in the USA has not even started yet, it just began as a curtain raiser in March 2020.

I have been blessed with a son in 2017.

I saw all this way back in March 12, 2003 itself when I did not know of the existence of the wonderful woman who I married in 2011 and with whom I have a son in 2017.

How did I see all this in March 12, 2003 when I was not even married and the war in Iraq had not even begun?

The main key to Happiness

The main key to Happiness is to do everything without expectations.

It is your right and prerogative to offer your love and sacrifice for someone.

Similarly, it is their right and prerogative to recognize that love and sacrifice.

This is extremely confusing.

You can offer love and sacrifice, sometimes for decades, and still not be recognized or even thanked and you cannot call the person who did not recognize it ungrateful.

You only have a right to accept, not a right to expect.

Is it right for you to expect?

Was it not just your duty to offer love and sacrifice for all that the other person had done for you in the past?

What I say is nothing new.

It is a fundamental precept of the Sanathan Dharma and is repeated many times in many of its scriptures.

The Gita says:

Be focused on action and not on the fruits of action.

Do not become confused in attachment to the fruit of your actions and do not become confused in the desire for inaction.

But what is action?

The Gita says:

He who sees inaction in action and action in inaction is wise among men.

Action means doing your duty without attachment to the fruits of your actions and always dedicated to Brahman.

You must do your duty regardless of what will happen to the results and without any expectation of the fruits of that action.

The Vishṇu Puraṇa says:

That is action, which does not promote attachment; that is knowledge which liberates.

All other action is a mere effort/hardship; all other knowledge is merely another skill/craftsmanship.

Apply this golden rule to every facet of your life and you will immediately drop the heavy baggage of expectations and all the associated disappointment that comes with it when your expectations are not met.

धर्म Dharma

The Rtam is the most absolute, perfect and divine law of Brahman.

Dharma along with Karma are the important and fundamental components of the Rtam.

There is no correct English translation of the word Dharma.

The closest meaning is a virtuous way of conduct and living but this is not even a 20% completely accurate nor comprehensive translation.

The Uttharkanda section of the Ram Charitra Manas has described Dharma in the most succinct manner that can be understood by all.

According to Lord Ram:

Brother, there is no greater Dharma than benevolence (परहति), no greater sin than oppressing others.

I have declared to you, dear brother, the verdict of all the Vedas and the Puranas, and the learned also know it.

Benevolence means altruism or selflessness and being always concerned about and working for the welfare of others.

परहति is a very complicated word.

A simpler meaning is निस्वार्थ सेवा or simply सेवा (SEVA). सेवा (SEVA) means Selfless Service.

So the highest Dharma is सेवा (SEVA) or Selfless Service not just to humanity, but to the whole world.

Because the highest ideal of the Sanathan Dharma is:

वसुधैव कुटुम्बकम् *(Vasudhaiva Kutumbakam)*

The whole World is One Family.

My description below may seem too long and lengthy and cumbersome.

Here is a concise description of the same by S Radhakrishnan, one of the greatest philosophers of modern Bharat.

What is Dharma?

If you understand hurting another man is adharma (violation of Dharma), pleasing another man is Dharma, you have performed Dharma.
S Radhakrishnan, 2nd President of India.

You do not need to learn any scripture or memorize any shlokas or perform any prayers and rituals, just practice the above words of S Radhakrishnan and you are an embodiment of Dharma.

Rule of Dharma is not only the right and responsibility of the "Hindu" religion.

It applies to every person of any religion.

Dharma is beyond religion.

It was created by Brahman.

And Brahman creates for all of creation, not just a particular religious group or for man alone.

The core essence of Dharma is:

धर्म एव हतो हन्ति धर्मो रक्षति रक्षितः ।

तस्माद्धर्मो न हन्तव्यः मानो धर्मो हतोवाधीत् ।।

Dharma defends those who defend it.

Dharma destroys those who destroy it.

Dharma can neither be created nor be destroyed.

You will reap what you sow.

Manu said:

Adharma (Iniquity), committed in this world, produces not fruit immediately, but, like the earth, in due season, and advancing by little and little, it eradicates the man who committed it.

Dharma, being destroyed, will destroy; being preserved, will preserve; it must never therefore be violated.

Most people who describe Dharma, especially new age peace and love gurus and even MK Gandhi himself spread the half-truth that Dharma is just Ahimsa (nonviolence), endless love and compassion.

Dharma is part of the Rtam.

The Rtam is the only supreme and divine law in this world.

The Rtam was created by Brahman.

And as we know Brahman is supremely patient, trusting and compassionate.

But as we also know the Rtam is dispensed dispassionately according to your Karma.

The whole verse from the Mahabharat is:

अहसिा परमो धर्मः
धर्म हसिा तथीव च
Ahimsa Parmo Dharma
Dharma Himsa Tathaiva Cha

Ahimsa(Non-violence) is the supreme Dharma,

So too is violence in service of Dharma.

Many volumes and books are written in all religions about the concept of Dharma.

According to these books, people follow Dharma by rituals, pilgrimages, prayers, sacrifices and appearances.

This confuses people.

According to other texts of the Sanathan Dharma including the Ram Charitra Manas, Dharma is composed of four basic pillars:

Truth
Purity
Charity
Compassion

Lord Ram also said:

Tolerance is a great virtue.

What is Truth?

Truth is that which is infinite and is eternal and it was never created but it always existed.

This is what Jiddu said about Truth:

There is no path to truth and there are no two truths.

Truth is not of the past or of the present – it is timeless – and the man who quotes the truth of the Buddha, of Shankara, of the Christ, or who merely repeats what I am saying, will not find truth because repetition is not truth: repetition is a lie.

Truth is a state of being which arises when the mind – which seeks to divide, to be exclusive, which can only think in terms of results, of achievement – has come to an end. Only then will there be truth.

The mind that is making effort, disciplining itself in order to achieve an end, cannot know truth because the end is its own projection and the pursuit of the projection, however noble, is a form of self-worship.

He alone shall know truth who is not seeking, who is not striving, who is not trying to achieve a result.

Jiddu also said the following about truth:

Truth is truth, one, alone; it has no sides, no paths; all paths do not lead to truth.

There is no path to truth, it must come to you.

Truth can come to you only when your mind and heart are simple, clear, and there is love in your heart; not if your heart is filled with the things of the mind.

When there is love in your heart, you do not talk about organizing for brotherhood; you do not talk about belief, you do not talk about division or the powers that create division, you need not seek reconciliation.

Then you are a simple human being without a label, without a country.

This means that you must strip yourself of all those things and allow truth to come into being; and it can only come when the mind is empty, when the mind ceases to create.

Then it will come without your invitation.
Then it will come as swiftly as the wind and
unbeknown.

It comes obscurely, not when you are
watching, wanting.

It is there as sudden as sunlight, as pure as
the night; but to receive it, the heart must
be full and the mind empty.

Now you have the mind full and your heart
empty.

Krishnamurti, J. Krishnamurti The Collected
Works Vol. V Benares, India 1949

What constitutes Purity?

Purity is constituted of heart, mind, body, and spirit.

That means there must be purity of thought, word, and action.

What constitutes Charity and Compassion?

Charity and Compassion are constituted by thought, word and deed.

Just throwing a few lakhs or even crores of rupees and putting your name on the donation board in front of the building does not really mean one is truly charitable and compassionate.

Charity and Compassion are only delivered by सेवा (SEVA benevolence), empathy and mercy.

Lord Ram also said in the Ramcharitmanas:

The conduct of the saint and the sinner is analogous to that of the sandal tree and the axe;
for - mark it, brother - the axe cuts down the tree, but the fragrant sandal imparts its perfume to the very axe that fells it.

For this reason sandal finds its way to the heads of the gods, while the axe, for its punishment, has its steel edge heated in the fire and beaten with a hammer.

In Section VI of the Shanthi Parva, Yudhishthira also describes other components of Dharma in addition to those above:
Forgiveness
Moderation and self-restraint
Renunciation and humility
Abstention from injury.
Injury does not mean just physical harm, but also the injury caused by feeling of hatred toward another person.

In addition to the above, the Gita also the mentions the following divine qualities:

Valour and Fearlessness
Wise apportionment of knowledge and Concentration
Sacrifice, Study of the scriptures
Austerity and Uprightness
Non-violence, Forgiveness, Fortitude
Tranquillity, Freedom from anger
Aversion to fault finding, Freedom from malice and excessive pride
Freedom from covetousness

Gentleness, modesty, and steadiness (absence of fickleness).

Consistently and constantly practicing the 3'Rs according to the Dalai Lama is also a part of Dharma:

Respect for Oneself
Respect for Others
Responsibility for Ones Actions

Another important component is:

Gratitude

Other aspects of Dharma will be practicing the things I have figured out, and also what I have written about Arya.

Learning the Dharma starts first at home, then in school and then in the village or town that you live in especially your immediate neighbourhood and among your family and friends.

Inculcation of Dharma can be greatly enhanced if one practices योग Yoga and ध्यान Dhyan daily.

Everybody wants to "conquer" the world.

We have great histories of world "conquerors" who only actually spread death and destruction.

It is more important to conquer yourself.

If you follow the above principles of Dharma you will conquer yourself.

As Paulo Coelho said: *If you conquer yourself, then you will conquer the world.*
NOTE:

There is no single person in this world, even the Gods themselves, who can always and faithfully follow all the principles of Dharma I have mentioned.

Even Lord Krishna instigated lies and deceit in the defeat of Bhishma and Karna.

Even Lord Rama shot Vali hiding from the back.

Sometimes people are forced into circumstances beyond their control and they violate some principles of Dharma.

But they still uphold Dharma if they follow at least 75% of the rest of its principles and make every effort in the future to correct and abide by the principles of Dharma that they have violated.

Dharma according to Lord Krishna

In the Gita, Lord Krishna teaches that Dharma is above everything.

If you have to break your vow to uphold Dharma, you should break it.

If you have to cheat to uphold Dharma, you should cheat.

If you have to kill your own wicked family to uphold Dharma, you should kill them.

Even a God, Lord Krishna broke his own vow, to save Arjuna who was fighting for the cause of Dharma.

Arjuna killed his own cousins, and even his revered granduncle Bhishma and his half-brother Karna to uphold Dharma.

I consider Lord Krishna the greatest upholder of Dharma, even more than Lord Ram.

This is because Lord Krishna upheld Dharma and did what was right, regardless of what others thought of him.

His instigated way of defeating of Bhishma and Karna was correct and done solely to uphold Dharma.

But it only bought him condemnation and a bad reputation because of the deceit involved in the way it was done, which was not befitting of the conduct expected by a Kshatriya.

But in the case of his banishment of Sita, Lord Ram upheld Dharma to do what others thought was right.

Sita had passed the Agni Pariksha.

There was nobody more pure-hearted and virtuous than her.

But to avoid the stigma of what other ignorant idiots thought of their queen, he banished her even though he knew in his heart that she was the most virtuous and pure-hearted of women.

Dharma according to Lord Ram

Lord Ram was called the Maryadda Purshottam – the most decent man and supreme embodiment of Dharma.

Yet when Vali and Sugriva were fighting, Ram shot Vali in hiding and from the back.

Vali was most disappointed and complained to Ram:

You are the Maryadda Purshotham, how can you shoot me in hiding, you should have come in front of me and shot me.

Then Lord Ram replied:

I am the Marayadda Purshotam only to people who are decent and follow Dharma.

You cannot claim to be decent after what you did to Sugriva, so I behaved with you as befitting an indecent man deserves.

But also remember this below about Lord Ram:

This is extract from an article by Sadhguru:

Ravana had ten heads.

Rama had to cut off all the ten heads to finally kill Ravana.

With the battle won, Rama said, "I want to go to the Himalayas and do penance, because I have committed a great sin.

I have killed someone who was a great devotee of Shiva, a phenomenal scholar, a great king, a generous man."

The others were shocked.

Lakshmana, his brother, said, "What are you talking about? He kidnapped your wife."

But Rama said, "Out of the ten heads of his, there was one that had great wisdom, piety, and devotion. I regret cutting off that head."

Further extract from the same article by Sadhguru:

What Rama was trying to say that no matter what horrible things Ravana had done, there was one aspect of him that was a tremendous possibility.

Just follow this fundamental principle - if you see something wrong in someone, condemn that, not the person.

If you bring this wisdom into your life, you will be free of baggage. When you do this to others, the same will happen to you.

Rama did penance for having killed a man who had kidnapped his wife and had done many other terrible things. Still, Rama identified this one head that was beautiful about him.

Rama was a man of great wisdom, which is why he is worshipped. He failed in many aspects *of his life, but his failures never altered his wisdom and quality.*

No matter what life did to him, he stayed above that.
I want you to remember Rama's example throughout the year.

If you are sensible enough to identify the quality rather than condemn the person, before Guru Purnima comes and we shift to Dakshinayana, or the southern run of the sun, you should have reaped a rich harvest.

A rose plant has more thorns than roses, but we still call it a rose plant because we recognize its beauty.

A mango tree has more leaves than mangoes, but we still call it a mango tree because we recognize the sweetness of its fruits.

Every human being has at least one drop of sweetness in them.

Why don't we see this?

Please do this with everyone around you – try to recognize that one drop of sweetness in even those people who you otherwise consider to be horrible.

Only if you recognize it in others, it will reflect in you.

On the other hand, if you see terrible things in other people, that is what will reflect in you.

This does not mean you should become blind to everything.

You see the leaves in the tree; you see the thorns in the rose bush - but you acknowledge the flower and the fruit.

Ram Rajya – The heavenly rule of Ram

People have no clue about the glorious acts of Lord Ram but want to live in Ram Rajya.

People ignorantly praise and clamour for Ram Rajya without understanding the sacrifice and dedication that went into building it.

Ram Rajya is not just the rule of Ram, it is the rule of Dharma of which Ram was the supreme embodiment.

Lord Ram followed Dharma, at all costs, even at the cost of sacrificing his wife, his unborn children and his ownself.

During Ram Rajya, not only Ram, but people themselves followed Ram and tread faithfully on the path of Dharma.

Here are some of the extracts of Ram Rajya from the Rama Charitra Manas of Tulasidas:

Rama's ascension to the throne brought joy to all the three spheres and ended all their sorrows. No one bore enmity to another; Rama's glory had obliterated all disharmony.(4)

Devoted to duty each according to his own caste and stage of life, the people trod the path of the Vedas and enjoyed happiness. They knew no fear, nor sorrow nor disease. (20)

No where in the kingdom was there anyone who suffered from affliction of any kind –

whether of the body, or proceeding from divine or supernatural agencies or that caused by another living being.
All men loved one another. Each conducted oneself in accordance with Dharma and were devoted to the precepts of the Vedas.(1)

Dharma with its four pillars (viz., truth, purity, compassion and charity) reigned everywhere throughout the world; no one even dreamt of sin. Men and women alike were devoted to Ramas's worship and all were qualified for final beatitude. (2)

There was no premature death nor suffering of any kind; everyone was comely and sound of body. No one was destitute, afflicted or miserable; no one was stupid or devoid of auspicious marks.(3)

All the men and women were unaffectedly good, pious and virtuous; all were clever and accomplished. Everyone recognized the merits of others and was learned and wise; All were grateful for kindness and the services and benefits received from others and were guilelessly prudent.(4)

Delight in these divine exploits is the reward of knowing his infinite greatness - so declare the greatest of sages and ascetics. The happiness and prosperity of Rama's reign were more than even Shesha (the serpent-god) and Sarasvathi (the goddess of learning) could describe.(3)

All were generous and charitable; men and women alike were devoted to the feet of the Brahmanas. Every husband was pledged to a vow of monogamy and the wives too were devoted to their husband in thought, word and deed.(4)

Throughout the realm of Rama, a rod (stick) was never seen save in the hands of the ascetics; the word "difference" too had ceased to exist except among the dancers in a dancing party. Even the word "conquer" was heard only with reference to the mind (for the only victory known was self-conquest).(22)

Trees in the forest blossomed and bore fruit throughout the year; the elephant and the lion lived together as friends. Birds and beasts of every description had forgotten their natural animosities and lived in the greatest harmony with one another.(1)

Birds sang and beasts fearlessly moved about in the woods in distinct herds, making merry all the time. The breezes breathed cool, soft and fragrant; bees hummed even as they moved about laden with honey.(2)

Listen, O king of the birds, during Rama's reign there was not a creature in this world, animate or inanimate, that was liable to any of the sufferings attributable to time, past conduct, personal temperament and character. (21)

Creepers and trees dropped honey to those who asked for it; cows yielded milk to one's heart's content. The earth was ever rich with crops; even in the Treta Yuga the conditions of the Sat Yuga prevailed.(3)

Conscious of the fact that the Ruler of the earth was no other than the Universal Spirit, the mountains brought to light their mines containing jewels of every description. Every river carried in it excellent water, cool, limpid and pleasant to the taste.(4)

The oceans kept within their bounds and scattered jewels on their shores for men to gather. Ponds were all thick with lotuses and every quarter(the whole nation) was clear and bright.(5)

The moon flooded the earth with her rays, while the sun shone just as much as was necessary. Similarly clouds poured forth showers for the mere asking so long as Rama was king.(23)

A mine of beauty, virtuous and modest, Sita was ever devoted to Her lord. She knew the greatness of the All-merciful Lord and adored His lotus-feet with a devoted heart.(2)

Although there were many man-servants and maid-servants in Her palace, all expert in the art of service, She did all household work with Her own hands and carried out the behests of Ramachandra.(3)

Sita invariably did what would afford delight to the All-merciful, conversant as She was with the art of service. Devoid of pride and conceit, She waited upon Kausalya and all the other mothers-in-law in the palace. (4)

Uma, (continues Lord Siva,) Sita was no other than Goddess Rama, the Mother of the universe, who is adored even by Brahma and other gods and is ever flawless.(5)

In every house the people recited the Puranas and narrated Rama's holy exploits of a diverse character. Men and women alike joined in hymning Rama's praises and days and nights passed on unnoticed.(4)

Not a thousand Sheshas(serpant Gods) could tell all the happiness and prosperity of the people of Ayodhya, where Rama reigned as King.(23)

All great sages like Narada, Sanaka and others came to Ayodhya everyday to have a sight of the Lord of Kosala, and forgot all their asceticism to the world the moment they saw the city,

with its attics built of gold and jewels and having splendid pavements laid in diverse colours. A most beautiful boundary wall with its battlements painted in different colours enclosed the city on all sides, as though the nine planets had mustered a large army and besieged Amaravati (Indra's capital). The ground (the streets and squares etc.,) was so beautifully paved with crystals of various colours that the mind of the greatest Sages would be enraptured at the sight.

The glistening palaces were so high as to reach the skies; their shining pinnacles put to shame as it were, the effulgence of the sun and the moon. Latticed windows made of diverse precious stones shone here and there; while every house was lit up with jewels that served as lamps.((1-4)

The mansions were illumined by jewels that served as so many lamps and had shining thresholds made of coral, pillars of jewels and walls of gold inlaid with emeralds, which were as lovely as though they had been built by the Creator (Brahma) himself.

Beautiful, charming and commodious as the palaces were, they had their courtyards inlayed with crystal, and every gate thereof was provided with doors of gold embossed with diamonds.

Everyone had a flower garden planted in a characteristic design and trimmed with the greatest care, in which beautiful and lovely creepers of every variety blossomed all the year round as in the spring season.

Bees hummed in a pleasant strain and a delightful breeze breathed cool, soft and fragrant. Birds of all kinds, reared by the children, sang in melodious notes and looked graceful in their flight.

Peacocks, swans, cranes and pigeons presented a most lovely sight on the houses, warbling and dancing in a variety of ways at the sight of their own shadow reflected everywhere (on the glossy surface of the roofs and balconies).

The children taught parrots and Mainas to repeat the words, Rama, Raghupati (the Lord of the Raghus), the Protector of His devotees.

The gates of the royal palace were magnificent in everyway; the streets, cross-roads and bazars were all splendid.(1-4)

The bazars were splendid beyond description; things could be had without any price there. How can anyone describe the wealth of the city where the Abode of Lakshmi Himself reigned as King?

The cloth- merchants, bankers and other dealers sat at their shops like so many Kuberas (gods of riches).

All men and women, children and aged folk alike were happy, all of good conduct and comely in appearance.

The best of all and beautiful in everyway was the royal ghat, where men of all the four castes could bathe.

All along the bank stood temples sacred to the gods and surrounded by lovely groves.(2)

The splendour of the city defied all description; its outskirts too were most picturesque. The very sight of the city with its groves and gardens, wells and ponds, drove away all one's sins.(4)

Its peerless ponds and tanks and charming and spacious wells looked so beautiful with their elegant flights of steps and limpid water that even gods and sages were fascinated by their sight.

The lakes were adorned with many-coloured lotuses and resounded with the cooing of the numerous birds and the humming of the bees; the notes of the cuckoos and other birds invited the wayfarers to rest in the delightful gardens.

Is it ever possible to describe the city of which Sita's lord was the King?

Anima (the power of assuming atomic size) and all other supernatural powers and even so joys and riches of every kind stayed in Ayodhya forever.

My dream for the next generation is that they achieve Ram Rajya where the law of Dharma is willingly and lovingly followed by all.

Bharat has all the potential to regain its historical wellbeing, fame, and glory.

But for Bharat to realise this, it has to abandon the fraud FUKUS based systems it has ruinously adopted and go back to our traditional heritage of Ram Rajya where the rule of Dharma was supreme.

My dream, at least for our generation, is for Bharat is to return to its greatness that was achieved during Magadha.

To start on this path we should first establish Law, the State and a team of Ideal Administrators of Bharat.

The path forward will be outlined in due course, and not just with my input, but with the input of all the real hard working and devoted people of Bharat.

Not the leeches who live off the fraud FUKUS systems of "democracy" and "capitalism" and suck the lifeblood out of the real hard working and devoted people of Bharat.

But the journey of a thousand miles begins with a single step. So, make the first step.

Twitter and Instagram #aryadharma #restorerealramrajya

Epilogue

Thank you for taking the time to read this book. It is much appreciated.

But your work is not done until you share this with your friends or at least publicise my website www.aryadharma.world among your friends and your social media accounts.

I have started writing the underlying concepts and registered my website www.aryadharma.org since 2006 without any expectation of a monetary reward but to change world consciousness and inspire people to understand the works of the great writers, monks and thinkers I have read and have tried to condense my life's research into a single book.

My main intention to write this book and the website www.aryadharma.world is to change world consciousness and governments to a better way of life and living and to restore the Arya Dharma – the Noble Dharma not only for humanity but for all beings in this world.

I still remember the golden words of my Dad's friend Mr Swami:

```
In the Vedanta, I find peace.
```

This small and profound sentence that I heard when I was a young child was spark for me to embark on my journey into finding peace and I wish to share with the world what I have found.

Dedication and Acknowledgements

I would first like to dedicate my work to Brahman with whose grace I was fortunate to be born to an educated, cultured and wealthy family, have good friends, relatives, colleagues, employees, education, jobs and be blessed with an intelligence, reasonable looks, health and a life of great privilege and comfort that probably less than 0.0001% of the people in this world have or could even aspire to in 7 lifetimes.

I would like to first sincerely thank my maternal Grandfather World War 2 Burma Star Medal winner Captain Bolakaranda Bopaiah Kutappa who raised me personally for the first 10 years of my life and formed the foundation of my character.

In memory of my grandfather and his risking his life to save his soldier's lives in World War 2 which earned him the Burma Star, I have chosen my pen name as Dhyan Kutappa Bollachettira while my official name will always remain Dhyan Appachu Bollachettira.

I would next like to sincerely thank my maternal Grandmother Dr Rosa Thomas who also laid the foundation of the character of my mother and whose dying dream of making her daughters doctors was made a reality by both my maternal grandfather and my mother and aunt.

I would next like to sincerely thank my paternal Grandfather Bollachettira Mandanna for being a role model to my father who inculcated not just in my father but in all his children the values of integrity, vision, appreciation of legacy and ancestral lands, hard work and devotion and love towards family.

I would next like to sincerely thank my paternal Grandmother Bollachettira Subbava who inculcated the love of farming, cows and value of hard work into my father at a very young childhood age.

I would next like to sincerely thank my mother Dr Sushila Appachu who gave birth to me, educated me and moulded me, laid the foundation of my character and has always been my role model of how an ideal woman as daughter, wife and mother should be with integrity, love, class, grace and unwavering dedication and support and selflessness towards her father, husband and children and the bringing the joy of parenthood to hundreds if not thousands of poor patients whose children she has brought into this world.

I would next like to thank my father Major (Retd) Bollachettira Mandanna Appachu for all his emotional, financial and educational support to me especially during my critical years in 2006 and also leaving behind to me a valuable legacy in the form of financial capital which I used to build my portfolio, and farms and agricultural lands that also include those which I live on and raise my family on.

I would also like to thank my father for his valuable contacts like ISKON and Mr Swami who first introduced me to the wonder of Vedanta by saying it brought him peace formed the fundamental basis for me to write this book.

Most of the books I read in my younger years like ISKONs Srimad Bhagavatam came from my father's library and most of my experiences in later years that I wrote in Things I have Figured Out came from interaction and learning from my father.

I would especially and sincerely like to thank my God given wife for her undying devotion, support and patience with me and her complete and unconditional love and acceptance of me despite all my faults and sometimes the hurt I caused her because of my stubbornness.

Among all the people I have met in this world, my wife is most like me.

Like me she is interested in values, not material interests.

Somehow destiny has brought us together and I would like to think we have found the keys to a successful marriage, though my wife may have a different opinion.

However, she has an advantage over me in these times because she is a realist and I am an idealist.

A realist sees things as they really are. An idealist sees things as they really should be.

I hope a day will come when idealists trump realists, but for now my wife's realism has saved me from disaster more times than I can remember.

I would especially like to thank my wife for willingly choosing to be one of the most important parts of my life and standing by me and having faith and immense patience in me despite all the troubles I have caused her.

I would next like to thank my sister for her love and support and also her family for their love and support.

I would also like to thank my in-laws, and immediate family for all they have done for me and for the fact that they always go out of their way just to make me happy.

I would also like to thank my nieces.

I would also like to sincerely than my God given miracle birth son who is my Living God and from whom I have relived the joys have childhood and who also reinforce my view that young children are the true face of Brahman.

I would also like to thank my closest friends, who are closer to me than many members of my family.

I would sincerely like to my neighbour who is an embodiment of Brahman to me and has been taking care of the most poor and helpless beings like abandoned stray dogs even at her advanced age.

I would also like to sincerely thank all those who worked for me and continue to work with me without whose help I would not have been to achieve anything much on my own.

I would also like to thank my colleagues at the various jobs I worked with and also my teachers and classmates at school and college.

I would also like to thank my pets and livestock from whom I derive simple and unblemished joy, sometimes much more than the humans I deal with including my family and who also reinforce my view that young animals, especially pets and livestock are the true face of Brahman.

I would also acknowledge some appreciation of those who caused me hurt either willingly or unwillingly, I may have not enjoyed my interaction with them, but I surely have learned from it and it made me a much stronger person.

Finally I would like to thank this great land of Bharat and all its people, especially in Bangalore and Kodagu, where I derive great joy every day and see great happiness and hope even among the poorest of people I deal with on a regular basis.

The real face of Bharat is poles apart of what both the domestic and foreign presstitute media portray.

For a good insight into all that is good and great and what is really going on in Bharat, read The Better India website.

www.ingramcontent.com/pod-product-compliance
Lightning Source LLC
Chambersburg PA
CBHW030625220526
45463CB00004B/1425